1,000,000 Books

are available to read at

Forgotten Books

www.ForgottenBooks.com

Read online
Download PDF
Purchase in print

ISBN 978-1-333-30364-8
PIBN 10486705

This book is a reproduction of an important historical work. Forgotten Books uses state-of-the-art technology to digitally reconstruct the work, preserving the original format whilst repairing imperfections present in the aged copy. In rare cases, an imperfection in the original, such as a blemish or missing page, may be replicated in our edition. We do, however, repair the vast majority of imperfections successfully; any imperfections that remain are intentionally left to preserve the state of such historical works.

Forgotten Books is a registered trademark of FB &c Ltd.
Copyright © 2018 FB &c Ltd.
FB &c Ltd, Dalton House, 60 Windsor Avenue, London, SW19 2RR.
Company number 08720141. Registered in England and Wales.

For support please visit www.forgottenbooks.com

1 MONTH OF FREE READING

at

www.ForgottenBooks.com

By purchasing this book you are eligible for one month membership to ForgottenBooks.com, giving you unlimited access to our entire collection of over 1,000,000 titles via our web site and mobile apps.

To claim your free month visit: www.forgottenbooks.com/free486705

* Offer is valid for 45 days from date of purchase. Terms and conditions apply.

English
Français
Deutsche
Italiano
Español
Português

www.forgottenbooks.com

Mythology Photography **Fiction** Fishing Christianity **Art** Cooking Essays **Buddhism** Freemasonry Medicine **Biology** Music **Ancient Egypt** Evolution Carpentry Physics Dance Geology **Mathematics** Fitness Shakespeare **Folklore** Yoga Marketing **Confidence** Immortality Biographies Poetry **Psychology** Witchcraft Electronics Chemistry History **Law** Accounting **Philosophy** Anthropology Alchemy Drama Quantum Mechanics Atheism Sexual Health **Ancient History Entrepreneurship** Languages Sport Paleontology Needlework Islam **Metaphysics** Investment Archaeology Parenting Statistics Criminology **Motivational**

Portrait by S. Van Hoogstraaten of Anne Finch, Viscountess Conway (?)
(The Royal Gallery, The Hague)

FINCH AND BAINES

A SEVENTEENTH CENTURY FRIENDSHIP

BY

ARCHIBALD MALLOCH

B.A. (Queen's); M.D. (McGill); Temporary Captain, Canadian Army Medical Corps

"Nulla dies unquam memori nos eximet aevo"
(Vergil as adapted by Finch)

Cambridge
at the University Press
1917

Portrait by S. Van Hoogstraaten of Anne Finch, V[iscou]ntess Conway
(The Royal Gallery, The Hague)

FINCH AND BAINES

A SEVENTEENTH CENTURY FRIENDSHIP

BY

ARCHIBALD MALLOCH

B.A. (Queen's); M.D. (McGill); Temporary Captain, Canadian Army Medical Corps

"Nulla dies unquam memori nos eximet aevo"
(VIRGIL as adapted by Finch)

Cambridge:
at the University Press
1917

TO MY FATHER
A. E. M.
A PUPIL AND DISCIPLE
OF
LISTER

PREFACE

AT the suggestion of Sir William Osler, Bt., F.R.S., Regius Professor of Medicine at Oxford, I undertook to write the story of the lives of Sir John Finch and Sir Thomas Baines, and it has been a very pleasant but quite a novel task.

The friendship of Sir John Finch and Sir Thomas Baines would make a very interesting psychological study for one qualified for such work, but I have endeavoured to give merely "a plain unvarnished tale," and as far as possible in their own words.

The material for this little work has been found largely in the Finch papers, a report on which is in course of publication by the Historical Manuscripts Commission, and in the letters of Finch and Baines to Anne Viscountess Conway at the British Museum. Certain useful facts have been gleaned from the *Calendars of Domestic State Papers* of the 17th century.

It is a pleasure to acknowledge my great indebtedness to Wilfred Finch, Esquire, the present owner of Burley-on-the-Hill, who has granted me permission to photograph and publish the portraits. Other members of the Finch family have also rendered valuable help in many ways.

My warmest thanks are due to Mrs Lomas, who is editing the *Finch Report* for the Historical Manuscripts Commissioners, for she has allowed me to take advantage of her wide experience; and to the Commissioners themselves for granting facilities for consulting papers in their custody. The second volume of the *Finch Report* is not likely to be published for some time on account of the War, but for convenience of reference I have been allowed to quote the pages of that volume on which letters used by me will appear.

I wish to express my gratitude to A. E. Shipley, Esquire, Sc.D., F.R.S., Master of Christ's College, for many kindnesses, and for permission to have a photograph taken of the tomb in Christ's College Chapel; to Dr Norman Moore for valuable suggestions; to Lionel Cust, Esquire, C.V.O., for help with the portraits and permission to use blocks made for the *Burlington Magazine* from my negatives; to Miss E. G. Parker, Oxford, for translations from the Latin; to Charles Baxter, Esquire, for translations of Italian letters; to the authorities in charge of the MSS. Room at the British Museum; to Miss J. Ogilvie, late of Somerville College, Oxford, for valuable aid in arranging the material; and to Captain W. W. Francis for help in reading the proof.

Also to Sir Wm. Osler I owe a great debt of gratitude for his influence, which has been a continual stimulus. I have gone to him in every difficulty that has confronted me in this work, and in spite of the immense demands on his time he has ever proved to be, as he has been called before, "the young man's friend."

A. M.

BRITISH EXPEDITIONARY FORCE, FRANCE
25th November, 1916

CONTENTS

CHAP.		PAGE
I.	Early Education	1
II.	Tour through France	5
III.	Education in Padua	10
IV.	Pisa	22
V.	England	30
VI.	Life in Florence	39
VII.	England again	56
VIII.	Constantinople	61
IX.	Death of Baines	71
X.	Return of Finch	77
XI.	Finch's Death, Burial and Will	79
	Appendix	83
	Index	85

LIST OF ILLUSTRATIONS

	PORTRAIT BY S. VAN HOOGSTRAATEN OF ANNE FINCH, VISCOUNTESS CONWAY (?)	*Frontispiece*
PLATE		
I.	FINCH'S ROOM AT CHRIST'S COLLEGE	*opposite p.* 3
II.	MONUMENTS TO BAINES AND FINCH IN THE AULA MAGNA, PADUA (*By kind permission of the Cambridge Antiquarian Society*)	,, 19
III.	SIR JOHN FINCH AT HIS STUDIES, BY S. VAN HOOGSTRAATEN	,, 21
IV.	PORTRAIT OF SIR JOHN FINCH	,, 31
V.	PORTRAIT OF SIR THOMAS BAINES	,, 32
VI.	PORTRAIT OF SIR JOHN FINCH, BY CARLO DOLCI	,, 51
VII.	PORTRAIT OF SIR THOMAS BAINES, BY CARLO DOLCI	,, 53
VIII.	MONUMENT OVER THE GRAVE OF FINCH AND BAINES	,, 79
IX.	WILL OF SIR JOHN FINCH	,, 80

CHAPTER I

EARLY EDUCATION

In the summer of 1915 a chance of this War placed me in charge of a small hospital for officers at Burley-on-the-Hill in Rutland. This was for years the seat of the Earls of Winchilsea and Nottingham, whose family name was Finch.

It is a house rich in historical associations and contains a large collection of fine portraits. Amongst these are several 17th century portraits of Sir John Finch and Sir Thomas Baines, which are apparently the only ones to be found in England. A valuable collection of family papers, many bearing on the lives of Finch and Baines, was sent to the Public Record Office several years ago together with note-books of these men.

Sir John Finch and Sir Thomas Baines probably hold an unprecedented record in history for close and unbroken friendship. They were both medical men and Fellows of the Royal College of Physicians and Fellows of the Royal Society in its early days. They numbered Henry More and other Cambridge Platonists amongst their friends, occupied important positions throughout their lives, and by their wills established themselves as great benefactors to Christ's College, Cambridge. In addition Finch was connected by marriage with William Harvey, the discoverer of the circulation of the blood.

Thomas Baines was the elder of the two friends, but of his family and early life we know very little except that he was the son of Richard Baines and was born at Whaddon in Cambridgeshire[1], was at school at Stortford under Mr Legh, and was admitted pensioner at Christ's College under Mr Gell, 5th October, 1638, when he was fourteen years of age. Reckoning from this the date of his birth must have been 1624, though it is commonly given as 1622. Two of Baines' brothers, Richard and Francis, had already been at Christ's College, having entered in 1622 and 1626 respectively. In the year 1642-3 Baines took his B.A. degree and in 1649 his M.A.

John Finch was the third son of Heneage Finch, Recorder of the City of London. John's eldest brother, Heneage, afterwards Lord Chancellor Finch

[1] See *Biographical Register of Christ's College* 1505-1905 by John Peile, and also *History of Christ's College* by the same author.

and first Earl of Nottingham, was born at Heneage House, but I have been unable to determine the place of birth of the second and third sons, Francis and John. According to F. Barnard's *Nativities*, a manuscript in the possession of Sir Wm. Osler, Bt., the date of John's birth was 15th March, 1626. He received his early education at Eton under Norris[1] and at Mr Sylvester's school in the parish of All Saints, Oxford.

The accounts of John Finch's university career are at variance; Anthony Wood[2] wishes to show that Oxford was Finch's first love, whilst Cambridge authorities do not like to relinquish any claim they have upon him. As Heneage Finch had already been at Oxford and as Sylvester was a Balliol man, it seemed probable that Wood was correct in stating that, at about the age of 15, Finch entered Balliol as a gentleman commoner. The complete Register of Balliol men never has been published, but the Rev. Andrew Clark, LL.D., Fellow of Lincoln College and now Rector of Great Leighs, Essex, has gone over all the registers (including the "buttery books") and I have been enabled to use his MS. which clears up the matter in question and shows that Anthony Wood's account is accurate. On 19th February, 1641-2, both Francis and John Finch, second and third sons of Sir Heneage Finch, Serjeant at Law, were admitted as fellow commoners to Balliol and both "gave £5 to Chapel Fund." In 1643 both men's names are on the books as fellow commoners; September, 1644, Francis' name does not appear though John is down as a fellow commoner but "non-resident": in 1645 and 1646 John Finch is still a fellow commoner and still "non-resident." During the latter year there were hardly any undergraduates, owing to the political disturbances, and John Finch's name is the only one given as fellow commoner. F. Barnard, Brit. Mus. *Sl. MSS.* 1683, gives a horoscope or "Astrology Scheme" of John Finch with several principal facts of his life. One interesting but very brief statement runs "sick at Newbury Fight," and this must refer to engagements in September, 1643, or October, 1644. Finch never mentions the Civil War, but Barnard's other statements are correct. Was Finch a combatant? In the year 1647, 22nd May, John Finch received the degree of B.A.

Finch's periods of non-residence at Balliol may be explained, for Joseph Foster in his *Alumni Oxonienses* states that Finch was admitted as member of the Inner Temple in 1644; however, both Francis and John (sons of Sir Heneage) were admitted in November, 1642[3], but only the former continued his studies there. John Finch sought a quieter spot than Oxford, then garrisoned by Royalist troops and where there was "scarce the face of an university left,"

---
[1] Peile, *loc. cit.*
[2] *Athenae et Fasti Oxonienses*, 2nd ed., Fasti 58.
[3] *Members admitted to the Inner Temple 1547-1660*, edited by W. R. Cooke, M.A., London, 1877.

Phot. J. Palmer Clarke

Finch's Room at Christ's College

so he went to Christ's College, Cambridge, and was admitted there as pensioner under Mr Potts, 11th April, 1645, at the age of 18 or 19. He returned to Balliol and obtained his B.A., 22nd May, 1647. Not knowing that Finch had first gone to Oxford, Peile found it difficult to explain why he took his B.A. at Oxford. However during this year Oxford "was turned topsy-turvy by the Visitors[1]" and Finch again went to Cambridge, and was incorporated in 1647 and had Henry More as his tutor.

At Christ's College Finch and Baines met and thus began their life-long friendship. The Book of Study Rents shows they were joint occupants of the "second upper chamber" in the "southermost" (? northernmost) staircase of the New Building, and Finch's arms are to be seen to this day in a finely oak-panelled room of the New, or Fellows, Building (Plate I). It is most probable that during Finch's second stage at Christ's College, he and Baines had Henry More, the Platonist (1614–1687), as their common tutor, though Gell, Baines' tutor, was still in residence; for Potts, Finch's former tutor, was no longer at Cambridge, having either died or been ejected, and many years later More claimed to have had them both under his care[2]. Both Finch and Baines wrote of him as tutor, and each left money to More in his will.

It is not quite so likely that More introduced the young men to each other, as is usually stated, though his relations with the family of Finch were possibly already intimate. His "Heroine Pupil," Anne, Viscountess Conway and Killutagh, was the eldest (?) child of Heneage Finch, Recorder of the City of London, and therefore sister to John Finch; and in later years More often visited her country seat of Ragley in Warwickshire. She was reputed the most learned of the "female metaphysical writers" of England. In the year 1676, More was persuaded by the Lord Chancellor, the Earl of Nottingham, to accept a prebend at Gloucester which however he immediately resigned to a friend[3]. John Finch, it would seem, "always retained a High Veneration for the Person and the Writings of the Doctor[4]."

In reference to the first meeting of Finch and Baines, Ward in his *Lives of the Professors of Gresham College* writes:

> They have a tradition at Christ College, that while Mr Finch was student there, taking too great liberties, his sizar Thomas Baynes, very tenderly admonished him of his misconduct: which at first he resented, but upon reflection complied with his advice, and ever after made him his constant and bosom friend.

Both Finch and Baines obtained the degree of M.A. at Cambridge in 1649.

---

[1] Wood, *loc. cit.*
[2] Epitaph on the tomb of Finch and Baines.
[3] Rev. R. Ward, Rector of Ingoldsby, *Life of Henry More*, 1710.
[4] Rev. R. Ward, *loc. cit.*

Dr George Rust[1] (d. 1670), who succeeded Jeremy Taylor as Bishop of Dromore (and ultimately was buried in the same tomb with Taylor), also belonged to the Cambridge Platonist School, and Henry More and John Finch were among his friends at Christ's College. Finch probably retained his friendship for Rust and the latter wrote a "Discourse of Faith" which was published by James Colli with the last edition of Joseph Glanville's *Lux Orientalis* (1682), a work on the pre-existence of souls, and was dedicated "to the Honourable Sir John Finch Knight[2]." Glanville was not a Cambridge man but was a follower of the Platonists, and this group of men at this time constituted a society for psychical research, so that Finch was probably not alone in some of his strange beliefs of which we shall speak later.

Soon after this date Finch and Baines left England to study medicine in Italy. About this time they wrote some verses in praise of the poems of Mr William Cartwright, "the most noted poet, orator and philosopher of his time," as Wood describes him. In 1651, eight years after Cartwright had died, at the age of thirty-two, a collection of his poems was published "ushered then into the world by many copies of verses mostly written by Oxford men[3]." Following some verses by "Fr. Finch, è Int. Templ.," comes the poem by his younger brother "Io. Finch," entitled "On Mr Cartwright's Excellent Poems," and very fittingly next in order come those by "Thomas Baines" entitled "Upon Mr Cartwright's Poems published after his death." Later on amongst the introductory verses are some by "Iz. Wa." The poems by Finch and Baines do not show much imagination in the matter, or great skill in the versification and are not worthy of much attention. To write verses of this nature was a very ordinary accomplishment in those days, but the poems merit passing notice, as the authors never published anything else either in prose or verse.

No verses by Baines appear in the Burley papers except some in Latin to Molinetti, but at the British Museum, in a collection of contemporary verses, there are several "extracted from MS. of Dr Baines" (*Addit. MSS.* 29921) and one of these poems is on friendship.

[1] *Dict. of Nat. Biog.*
[2] Wood, *Athenae Oxonienses*, 2nd ed., vol. II, p. 665.
[3] "*Comedies Tragi Comedies with Other Poems, by Mr William Cartwright*, late Student of Christ Church, Oxford." London, printed for Humphrey Moseley, 1651, octavo. Selden's copy, to which Wood refers, is in the Bodleian Library.

CHAPTER II

TOUR THROUGH FRANCE

Finch and Baines determined to study abroad, but Andrich's[1] book on the English and Scottish students at Padua does not give their names until 1654–5. However a pass to travel into France was granted in 1651, as the *Calendar of State Papers* for that year shows, and the intervening period is well covered by the Conway papers (Brit. Mus. *Addit. MSS.* 23215) and by a journal written by John Finch which has been published amongst the Finch papers by the Historical Manuscripts Commission[2]. It deals with their visits to "Diepe," Rouen, Paris and their passage through Sens, Dijon, and Lyons to Geneva. The journal is cut off short before they reached Milan. It begins "Wee set out from London October 20, 1651. Tuesday 21, we came to Rye, with my sister C[onway] and brothers C[onway] and F. F[inch]." This young man John Finch kept his wits about him, and his eyes and ears open, and was not taken in by some sly thieves. He grows delightfully gossipy at times, especially about "Sir K. D[igby]," whom he knew in Paris. In a thin vellum bound book, which was amongst the manuscripts of Finch and Baines at Burley-on-the-Hill, there is on the front page a small table of accounts dated "Paris December 17th 1651."

From a medical point of view some passages in the journal are quite worth quoting. Speaking of Rouen, he says, "It is the biggest city in France next to Paris unlesse Lyons stand in competition with it. But it is seldome free from the plague by reason that it is encompassed on every side with hils, so that the aire is not free." They reached Paris Sunday, November 9–19

---

[1] *De Natione Anglica Et Scota Juristarum Universitatis Patavinae*, Scripsit *Io. Aloys Andrich, Patavii* MDCCCXCII —Caput v. Scholares Anglici p. 148. "MDCLIV-V d. Ioannes Finchi anglus allias 21": "d. Thomas Banes anglus allias 22." On p. 150, in a long list of names, we find "d. Thomas Baines anglus allias d. Ioannes Fineck anglus allias." This latter is one of the few instances in which the usual order of names is reversed. It will be seen that both names suffer changes and on p. 151 there is written "d. Thomas Bain anglus allias." For "allias" read "otherwise" or "entered elsewhere also" as the names are given in the New Register. It is seen here and later on p. 18 that the bedell of the University made many mistakes in writing down the names, and the Latin endings are marvellous.

[2] *Report on the Manuscripts of Allen George Finch Esq. of Burley-on-the-Hill*, vol. 1 (cd. 6508), 1913, p. 59. Also see letter from John Finch to his sister Mrs Conway, *Calendar of State Papers—Domestic Series* 1651-1652, p. 205, which describes incidents of his trip from Paris to Lyons.

and remained there till March 14. He compares the city with London and writes:

> The streets are more durty (*sic*) than London, yet one may walke cleaner because the streets are better paved...and though Paris is situated so low and all the filth of the houses emptied into the streets, yet the plague is very rarely amongst them; but the diseases (which) are most frequent are the dropsy, shed stone and fievres. And the Paris physitians, be the disease what it will, always open a veine and praescribe a ptisan and a purge of manna.

Speaking of the Carthusians, he says they

> are nigh to this [Palais de Luxembourg] who, though they never eat no flesh, yet feed upon macreus (macreuses, Scotch barnacles). They do not allow Bezar[1] because the stone of goats, nor any medcin comming from flesh in any case. To study chymistry is forbidden by their statutes as Father Mignet told me. They pray at least 11 hours in the 24, so that they have little time to study.

His picture of the conditions obtaining in the hospitals is a striking one.

> The Hostel Dieu for the number of diseased is a famous hospital but there's eight in a bed. But the Charité is the best accomadated that can be, as well as any gentleman in his own house. I believe there is about 200, every man in a bed singly. The paynes of those religious persons, which tend them is to be pitied.

From Paris they proceeded to Sens and thence to Auxerre, Noye (Noyers), Dijon, thence to Chalon.

> To Chalon we came Aprill 6. which wee had as little time to see as Beaune (a pretty town where there's the best hospital of France). In Chalon the Prince of Condé has a small but pretty house, and the Nostre Dame de Chalon is famous for miracles before whose shrine I saw many crutches hanged up which they say were the *vota* of the healed....On Sunday April 4-14 for 18£, I took horse with the messenger for Geneva (*i.e.* from Lyons) but so extreamly sick that I was, besides asthmaticall, generally distempered.

Whilst in Geneva he writes "on Wednesday, Aprill 7-17, I came to the house of Monsieur Parost that married a Welch woman; he was steward to Monsieur Beleivre the French Embassadour. In three dayes, finding English beere and conveniences, after a purge I was perfectly well."

It is very much to be regretted that this journal was not kept constantly throughout Finch's stay in Italy. However the journal is well supplemented by the letters from Finch to his sister which are to be found in manuscript amongst the Conway papers at the British Museum[2]. These letters are of the most affectionate nature and show a real love of Finch for Anne Conway. There must have been a constant interchange of epistles between the brother and sister almost every week up to the time of her death in 1679; but only one in this series from Anne to John is preserved. Some of the letters are written to "Dearest Soule," but the favourite term of address is "Dearest Dear" or "My D.D." They close usually with the words "Your most entirely affectionate Brother."

---

[1] *Lapis bezar*, supposed antidote for poison (note in report on MSS.).
[2] Brit. Mus. *Addit. MSS.* 23215.

Writing from Paris December 1–11, 1651, he makes an interesting note about Calvin:

As I went by the Colledge Moyen built by Cardinall Moyen I saw the house which Calvin liv'd in, it is in the close to the Colledge but it is pull'd down to the ground and none suffer'd to build upon (the) place any more; which is punishment inflicted upon none but the worst of malefactors as upon Ravilliac a schollar of the Jesuits who stab'd Henry the 4th. But Calvin's house is now made a Dunghill.

In these letters Dr Harvey is mentioned several times and perhaps it is better to group together at this point the passages referring to him, although the two last are from letters of a little later date. Heneage Finch married Elizabeth, daughter of William Harvey's younger brother Daniel, and the relations of the two families must have been quite intimate. At Burley-on-the-Hill were kept for many years the "tabulae Harveianae" which are dry specimens of human blood vessels and nerves. In 1823 they were presented to the Royal College of Physicians, by the Earl of Winchilsea[1], and only about ten years ago portraits of Dr Harvey, Mrs Harvey and of Sir Daniel Harvey were lost in a fire at Burley. The wills of Finch and Baines were put into the hands of Dr Harvey's brother, Sir Eliab Harvey (*vide infra*). William Harvey's last will was signed in the presence of Heneage Finch and Francis Finch and he left to his "loving cousin, Mr Heneage Finch for his fair pains, counsel and advice about the contriving of this my will one hundred pounds."

In the letter from Paris just quoted Finch gives a remarkable story of Harvey which I do not think has ever been published before.

I was on Saturday with Sir Kenelme Digby where I had some philosophicall Discourse; and he had heard of your marriage, but wondered with me at the story of Dr Harvey; I must confesse I have scarce faith enough to beleive (*sic*) that he would Cutt himselfe but rather beleive he voyded that stone you spoke of then cutt it out for I doe not see it was possible for him in two dayes to be able to goe abroad otherwise.

Although by this time Harvey was an old man, Anne Conway, who was a life-long invalid, was evidently under his care; for Finch writes from Geneva, August 1–10, 1652:

I grieve much you are not yet dearest out of Dr Harvey's hands for though he is as able a person as any I know, yet I had rather you had no reason for him to exercise his skill which I wonder hath been so long time with so little success.

Finch, though he had not yet begun the study of medicine at any university, does not hesitate to finish his letter with a great deal of advice as to his sister's health.

A year later this young man again takes an independent stand in another

---

[1] Munk's *Roll Call of the Royal College of Physicians*, vol. 1, p. 144. See p. 36, and also Appendix.

matter. He writes to his brother-in-law Conway from "Padoua, October 20-30, 1653," to the following effect:

As to the Question whether there be any such thing as an Universall Medicine or not, tis a thing I should not like be brought to speak of under any Notion but that of affection; for I am so conscious to my selfe of my owne weaknesse that the commendations of Dr Harvey and my other friends were a strong argument for my silence that I might not forfeit their good opinion by appearing much below their apprehension: but the motives to say something being the joynt desire of my sister and yourselfe; either of which wholy dispose of me, to show both my obedience and affection I have added what follows.

Finch's opinion of this "Universall Medicine" will be learnt later. It seems very possible that Finch knew Harvey personally and that Harvey suggested to him that he should go to Padua to study medicine.

Whilst in Paris, Finch wished his letters addressed "à Monsieur Jean Finch Gentillhomme Anglais, demeurant à la maison de Mademoiselle Beaumarché, en la Rüe Morfondüe, près la Porte de Sainct Marceau à Paris."

Writing from Geneva, Finch gives his sister a description of the town, and in speaking of the Lake tells her the tragedy of a man of science, whose religious beliefs brought him to his death—the story of Servetus.

There were two here executed for religion much talked of whose story I would not have you ignorant of; One Servetus a great Schollar in his time but of the same opinion which Socinus after divulg'd. He wrote to Mr Calvin concerning these points, who desired him to come to Geneva and he would give him a safe convoy. Servetus came, but instead of disputing the buisenesse if he might receive satisfaction, Mr Calvin found him obstinate and Servetus thought to have returned into Italy whence he came but he was accused to the Councell by Mr Calvin as an Apostate from Christianity and so burnt.

It is quite interesting to note that Finch does not mention Servetus' discovery of the lesser circulation of the blood (*i.e.* from the heart through the lungs and thence back to the heart), but this was hidden away in the midst of a theological treatise by Servetus entitled *Christianismi Restitutio*, 1553.

Finch gives the tale of the other martyr, but the letter is defective and some of the words are torn out.

...[*First word torn and gone*] Anton[io] since Mr Calvin's time was a Man that studied the Civill Law, at length he ...ld have chang'd his Religion and turn'd Jew. The Jewes would not admit him in the Synagogue, he lived at Nancy in Lorrain, and found to be of the Religion and [w]as and recommended to be Parson of Versoy a town upon the Lake a mile [from] Genève he Preach'd there a year and the Lord of the Town a scollar, observ'd he never made no mention of Jesus Christ and so begun to Question his faith which he find...one night in his shert came in the snow to Genève where being stopt by the Guard he told them that he was a Jew and that that was the only Religion...be sav'd...and that he would wish them to become so, he was committed to Bed[lam]...[*torn*] being not mad was Condemn'd to be burnt as he went to the sta[ke]...[*torn*] out of a cloud which he took for a Miracle and exhorted all the People to be Jewes and spoke many blasphemous words and so di[ed]. Dearest I begin to find my paper draw to an end and therefore I must come to a conclusion.

These letters as a rule contain some affectionate messages to Conway and to Henry More: "present my humble service to Mr More and excuse my not writing to him which you may justly do since I have scarce time to end this but that I am rejoysed to lay aside all things in order to you..." and neither Finch nor Baines forgets to send remembrances to "Mrs Sarah," Anne Conway's "library keeper," so that in all probability they had stayed with the Conways before they left England. John Worthington (1618–1671) was a friend of More and Anne Conway. In his will he left to several people "20s. to buy a ring"; amongst them was his niece "Sarah Worthington." It seems very probable that "Mrs Sarah" and his niece were one and the same person.

CHAPTER III

EDUCATION IN PADUA

Finch and Baines reached Padua in due course and began the study of medicine, but their letters give us little idea of the life at the University at that time, or of their particular work. Anne Conway was instructed to send letters "al Georgio il Bedello-della natione Inglese." Baines was very fond of writing descriptions of the trees and fruits of the country and of comparing them with those of England. The weather also interested him greatly at times; their first winter was cold, and he wonders much at this when he hears that the season was a warm one in England:

> Surely wee may justly expect a distemper in this great animal the World, when shee is so praeternaturally cold in these parts neere the heart, the sunne I mean, and so unreasonably warme at the very same time in her extremities.

In Finch's letters to his sister there are some interesting passages about the alchemist Van Helmont, the younger. In later years Van Helmont spent much of his time at Ragley and indeed was there when Anne Conway died, but at this time she was seeking everywhere a cure for the headaches that troubled her so much throughout all her life, and she wrote to John Finch about Helmont and his universal medicine as she wished to cross over to Holland to consult him. Finch replied to her enquiries in October, 1652:

> ...I shall again to fulfill your desires tell you my thoughts on all the Particulars you mention. I told you our Anatomy Professor, a Venetian, informed me that Ottho Janckenius was dead, but upon further enquiry I was the day after I sent away my last inform'd he was alive. Whereupon I wrote a long Latin letter to him to know whether he was the Person that sett out Van Helmonts workes assuring him that then I would wayt upon him to know whether he knew any great cures effected by young Helmont, and particularly in the headach, or whether he knew young Helmont pretended to an Universall Medicine. To all which he returned me a civill reply in Latin and told me he was that man sett out that edition of Van Helmont, but as for cures effected by Helmont at Venice, he knew none though he was intimate with the young man, except a feavour after Nature had made the Orifis by Antimony fixed, which saith he, was owed rather to Nature than his Ars, nay sayth he to speak, as I ought, in a matter of so great importance: He is a very ignorant Person and though I have diligently observed him I never knew him speake or doe anything extraordinary.
> I told my Brother Conway in my last that young Helmont had done two Cures on feavours as Moretus the Mathematique Professor told me but Jackening knowes but of one he tells me and that was done by Nature to the young mans hand. I enquired of a German concerning him and he told me that five of them Drs in Physick made it their businesse to know what [gr]eat matters had been effected by Helmont but that they found Nothing in

all their...[torn] [w]orth mentioning save that at Augusta invited to dinner by a Margrave he [and the M]argrave both dranke themselves sick, and that he then gave Physick to the Margrave which had like to have lost him his life whereupon the friends of the Margrave had killed him but that the Margraves Confessour carried him out of the Citty upon his own Horse young Helmont riding behind him for his security.

I told you last weeke of two persons cured by Sir Ken. Digby whom the Father had not cured and therefore the Father himselfe had no such universall remedies, he having described five hundred besides that universall, which were it effectuall the use were superfluous. I added that neither Helmont nor any man living ever pretended to cure all sorts of Tumors and Ulcers by the same medicine; but that which heales one Gangrenes another and inward diseases arising from the same cause which outward doe tis impossible to cure them by the same medicine unlesse somebody can assure Mee that he can Cure a Cancer by the same remedies he does bring a Phlegmon to suppuration, or that cold and hott distempers are both cured by the same things: which if any man thinkes he may reconcile all the Contrarieties in nature, it being impossible to introduce a disease because the same thing that causes it would at the same time be its Cure.

Van Helmont sayes that one Butler, an Irishman, had this Universall Medicine. I am sure I never in all my life time heard one word of Any such man. indeed there was a Butler at Cambridge a rare man but he had none of those secrets I am sure Or else Crane his Apothecary had never gotten £1500. per annum by his bills. Things return in a Circle wee admire them beyond sens and they us and to speake freely my Dearest I never yet found any thing since my travell Equall to the Report I have heard made of it but all men have a levity of spirit upon them to extoll and increase what pleases them and diminish what they dis...[torn]. If you would have me speake plainly to you, Helmont shall alwayes be more prized where he is not, than where he is....

Finch continues that the voyage itself to the Low Countries may do his sister good even if there Van Helmont can achieve nothing. Helmont at this time is always treated with scant courtesy by Finch who determined to go and see him in Germany:

Since that I am told by two Gentlemen of Bruxells that young Helmont is not there, but that he is at this Present with the Elector of Luxenburgh at Sarisburgh, some two dayes journey from Trent, and about five dayes journey from Padoua: so soone as I am assured of this which I expect this night or tomorrow: Mr Baines and I will make a journey thither on purpose.

Soon after this Finch and Baines made a short tour to Milan and Bologna, and writing from Padua, December 4–14, 1652, after their return, he tells how he sought there to cure Anne of her headache and at the same time reveals the fact of his superstition.

The Church of St Peter the Martyr is observable, Aquinas wrote a copy of verses as he passed that way for his epitaph, under the canopy of his tomb there are three coffins of Marble which if one kisses they are free from the headache, your servant and I kissed them on your behalf; I wish the remedy may succeed....

It is generally stated that Finch was Consul of the English nation at the University of Padua; but this seems hardly likely in view of the manner in which he expresses himself on this point in 1652:

My Dearest, Mr Baines wrote thee word I refused to be Consull of the English Nation at Padova although I was so importuned to it that I was afraid of being forced unlesse I had prevented it by a design, I doe assure thee twas impossible for me to have had that office unlesse I would have been drunk at least 40 times in the year.

At this time (1652) Finch began to send to his sister and brother-in-law long "Discourses" on philosophical and scientific subjects. In one of these "discourses" there is a very curious account "Of the Manner by which Trees Plants and all Vegetables are Nourished." It begins with the extraordinary statement that "Trees and plants are nourished not by the Root but by the Bark," and closes with an interesting passage:

> If it be urged further that Plants are Nourished by the Root because that In the Spring and Summer their sap rises, and in the Winter it falls, which those that sell timber precisely observe and therefore sell it in September, and likewise at the full of the Moon the sap rises more than in the wain: and hence Physitians in their praescriptions in the Winter time alwayes prescribe Roots and in the Spring time the Leaves but not in the Autumne. To this I must reply that in those Creatures where there is a perfect circulation of the blood wee discern the same effects and that the sap does not circulate by comming from the barke to the Root.
>
> In our selves we find that Vomits worke more in the Spring then Winter, That wee are subject to sweating, That our brain and all our humours doe increase and decrease with the Moone: But more particularly, Beares all the Winter long sleep in their Dens and eat nothing when the sap is, as it were, driven to the Root, but in the Spring when the Sun has its new vigour they, like plants, have their Resurrection and yet there was in them, shutt in their dens, the same circulation there was before and after, although not so vigourous in the one as to keep them wakeing nor in the Plants as to keep them flourishing. Tortoises Cuckows and swallows and all sorts of Insects as Flies bees etc. are nipt by the Winter and like Plants have their sap retire to their Root for they show forth no Exteriour Vitall Actions, but at the Spring they show by their singings and Motions they are newly reviv'd as well as Plants by their buds, and to speake truth what the heart is in sensitive Creatures the same thing is the basis in a Plant, and the driving of the sap to the Root is the same which the diminution of Naturall heat is in an Animall which hath sense, and its necessity and goeing underground for shelter.
>
> Lastly it moves me much to be of this Opinion what I and Mr Baines observed in passing Mount Sampion, Wee saw a Firr Tree grow out of the Top of a great peice of a Rock which had fallen down nay it grew out of the very Top of the Stone as if it had risen out of a Table, so that there was not the least imaginable Earth which could give it Nourishment, so that of Necessity it must be Nourished from its tender Tops of the branches and indeed upon all those hills there is nothing but continued Rocks of stone and yet no place can be fuller of Trees.

Harvey's book *Exercitatio Anatomica De Motu Cordis et Sanguinis in Animalibus* was published at Frankfort in 1628, and any references to the circulation within 25 years after this date are always full of interest—as they show the growth of an idea. In his argument Finch observed part of the truth but depends too much upon analogies between vegetable and animal life.

Finch writes from Venice 10–20th February, 1652–3, about the "Discourses"; his sister was evidently stimulating the young man in his studies:

> You may thinke dearest that I have fayled your expectation in that I have not sent you any discourse of consequence, seriously I have severall on the Anvill, and I cannot finish

any yet fitt for you to read, for I shall study for your satisfaction as much as my own....
Pray present my services to Mr More and let me know what he insists on in his booke and the dedication to you.

There was later great consternation and much writing about one part of these "Discourses" which miscarried in 1667, but fortunately Finch had numbered the pages and kept a copy. Thus he was able to transcribe it, although he complained of the length of time required to do this. For many years Finch kept up this practice of sending these essays to England. Henry More, in his letters to Anne Conway, writes of the discourses which she had sent on to him to read.

As early as the year 1651-2 Finch was interested in Descartes and writes to Anne Conway (vide *Cal. Dom. Papers* for that year):

...I sent you 3 of Descartes *Principles* [Amsterdam 1644] by Mr Ayres, and hope you have sent 2 to Cambridge and kept the 3rd for yourselfe. There was another MS. which will do you no harm to peruse...if you are in your Mathematicks.

Henry More devoted many years of his life to the study of Descartes, and although at first he looked on it very favourably, in later years he severely criticized Descartes' Natural Philosophy. Finch in the following criticism is chiefly concerned with Descartes' mathematics. It is expressed in a letter in May, 1658:

...As to Descartes my Dear I would with all my heart that I could thinke his Philosophy as true as coherent: but coherency is no argument for he must be a man of mean parts, that forgetts himselfe so far as to make one deduction contradict another. In short, most of Descartes I looke on as the old Philosophy in new names....

Finch and Baines only mention one of their teachers at Padua and this was Molinetti, the Professor of Anatomy. In 1649 he succeeded Veslingius in the chair which had been occupied by Vesalius, Fallopius and Fabricius ab Aquapendente. He was the author of *Dissertationes anatomico-pathologicae*, Venet. 1675, 4°, and in this same year was the first to operate on the antrum of Highmore through the cheek[1]. He was distinguished in the practice of medicine and also is said to have discovered the seventh of the group of extrinsic muscles of the eye[2].

In one of his note-books Finch copied out a very curious Latin poem which might have been composed by one of the Mystics. It was written by Baines in praise of this Venetian Molinetti, and is headed by the words: "Charissimi Thomae Baines equitis Aurati / Carmina in Anatomicas Molinetti / dissectiones Patavii Publice peractas / ab Antonio Molinetto rei Anatomicae primario professore, 1652."

[1] Haeser, *Lehrbuch der Geschichte der Medizin*, Bd. II, S. 692.
[2] Bayle, *Biographie Médicale*, T. II, p. 20.

Stupenda vidimus! et quod est stupendius
Quot carnis offae, quot concisa frustula,
Tot extiterunt veritatis martyres.
Qui ne sepulchro destituantur nobili
Fiamus urnae comites atque has reliquias
Tanquam sacra Naturae servemus, ut brevi
Tot sint sepulchra quot vivorum pectora.
Molinette sic decet queis admoves manum
Tractare corpora, quamvisque sint emortua,
Peccamus, ulterius si pateremur mori.

Sed filiorum sentias clemens Pater
Dulces querelas, quas vagientes proferunt.
Ænigmaes omnes solvis, et nectis nodos.
Desinimus admirari hominem, at novus labor:
Incipimus unum obstupescere Molinettum.
Qui flexuosos sanguinis dum tramites
Agilemque cursum permeatus lubricos
Scrutaris, en sanguis correptus extasi
Stat piger in venis, nescitque progredi
Quia cum stupore viderat motum suum.
Sic pertinaces improbamus omnia.
Cur? quippe quod Tu luculentius probas.

Dissectiones laudent quèis placent tuas;
Parcius oportet istas: nam me judice
Non dissecas Molinette sed adornas corpora;
Et sordibus remotis, in crus integrum
Producis in Theatrum, et sequaces musculi
Solvuntur ad tactum; sic non Te Anatomicum
Praestas sed id quod abunde magis est, Deum.

Natura olim prodigiorum frusta parens
Effaeta quorsum monstra non cudis nova?
Nubes fugantur, lacteae fulgent viae,
Chylumque priscam molientem fugam
Molinettus intercepit, et thalamis tuis
Saepe salientem deprehendit sanguinem
In circulare motu: et ille publice
Ostendit arcanum prorsus connubium[1]
Arteriarum cum venis, ut oscula
Fixere dulcia, mutuisque amplexibus
Laetantur indies, unde emersit Tua
Numerosa proles tot per elapsa saecula[2].

Vesica duplex, musculus monstrum triplex
Nihil valebant, risit ad minutias:
Age igitur ô Potens Dea! res urget novi
Locare statim corporis fundamina.
Novos vocamus ductus et vitae nova
Principia; quod dignus est majoribus
Molinettus ausis et meliori carmine.

[1] "Hae Anastomoses manifestissimae sunt, in Vasis praeparantibus et plexu choroide."
[2] "In illa dissectione monstrabat duplicem vesicam. Et musculus brachii biceps erat Triceps."

Which might be translated:

Poems of the most beloved Sir Thomas Baines, Knight, on the anatomical dissections publicly performed by Antonio Molinetti, Professor primarius of Anatomy, at Padua, 1652.

We have seen stupendous things, and, what is more stupendous, as many were the morsels of flesh, as many as were the clean-cut fragments, so many witnesses of Truth appeared. And that these may not lack an honourable sepulchre, let us become companions to the funeral urn, let us preserve these things as sacred things of Nature, so that, in short there may be as many graves for them as there are breasts of living men. Thus, Molinetti, it behoves us to treat the bodies to which you apply your hand, and, dead though they may be, we should sin should we suffer them to die again.

But hear, kind Father, the gentle complainings of thy children, which they lisp forth. You solve all enigmas, and you weave knots. We cease to wonder at man; but a new labour arises: we begin to be amazed at Molinetti alone. While you search the supple pathways of the blood, its nimble course, its slippery passages, behold our own blood seized with ecstasy, halts inert in our veins, and cannot advance, because it had seen with wonder its own motion. Thus we obstinately blame everything. Why? Because you prove too lucidly.

Let those to whom they are pleasing praise your dissections. These things should be done more sparingly; in my judgment, you do not dissect bodies, Molinetti, but adorn them. You bring them into the Theatre cleansed from all dirt, perfect in limb, and the obedient muscles are freed at your touch; thus you show yourself not an anatomist, but, what is far greater, a god.

Nature, who was formerly the parent of prodigies, why art thou now exhausted, why dost thou not shape new monsters? The clouds are dispersed, the milky ways shine forth; Molinetti intercepts the chyle as it endeavours to continue its ancient flight, and often he stays the blood as it issues from thy chambers in its circular course: and he shows publicly the secret marriage of the arteries[1] with the veins, how they exchange sweet kisses, and rejoice daily in mutual embracements, whence has arisen thy numerous progeny throughout past ages.

A double bladder[2] and an unnatural triple muscle were of no use, he laughed at such trifles: come therefore, oh mighty goddess, it behoves at once to lay the foundations of a new body. We call for new ducts and new principles of life; Molinetti is worthy of greater deeds and a better song.

In those days teachers of anatomy used public demonstrations as Harvey did in England in his Lumleian Lectures. Pepys in his *Diary*, 27th February, 1662–3, gives a very interesting description of the whole ceremony of such a demonstration as he saw it some years later. The "theatre" which Baines refers to is probably the one erected in Padua in 1593 by the Seigneury of Venice as a tribute to Fabricius, when thirty years of his professorship had passed.

Bound together with the letters of Henry More to Anne Conway, which were bequeathed to the British Museum by the Hon. John Wilson Croker in 1860,[3] is a small slip of paper on which is written an account of the circulation of the blood. It is undated and unsigned and there is no reference to the document in the next letter, which bears the date 23rd March, 1666–7. But it is in the hand of John Finch and resembles most closely his writing between the years 1653 and 1663. At this period he was more concerned with the study of Anatomy than in later years. In the year 1661, Malpighi with the aid of the

---

[1] "These anastomoses are most manifest in the vessels of preparations and in the choroid plexus."
[2] "In that dissection he showed a double bladder, and the biceps of the arm was a triceps!" These notes are by Baines or Finch.   [3] Brit. Mus. *Addit. MSS.* 23216.

microscope discovered how the blood reaches the small veins from the terminal arteries. But since Finch does not make use of this new knowledge, we must assume that his account of the circulation was written before that date.

He ranges himself on the side of Harvey, but it is interesting to note relics of the pre-Harveian idea that the blood ebbed and flowed in both the arteries and veins. It took time for men to follow up the Master's doctrine to all its definite conclusions. The heart lies at the point of contact of two circles, the greater and lesser vascular systems, and the blood flows only in one direction in the blood channels. Finch makes use of the expression "into all the arteries *from* the body," when in reality he knows that the blood in the arteries always flows from the heart *to* all parts of the body. He shows a similar lack of definiteness in his description of the veins, for he speaks of their being "*diverted into* the whole body," instead of saying that the blood flows *from* the whole body and is gathered up in two great veins.

Galen regarded the liver as the centre of the venous system and to this view Finch would seem to adhere, if it is forgotten that we are all slaves to words and phrases. In science traditional descriptions of *structures* are often retained, though our knowledge of their *function* may have greatly advanced. Now-a-days text-books of Anatomy often describe the course of nerve fibres or tracts, in a manner irrespective of the direction, in which Physiology teaches us, the impulse travels. Thus the subject is made more difficult for the student than if structure and function were taught at one and the same time.

Of the Circulation of the Blood.

The Circulation of the Blood is the passing of the Blood from the heart into the Arteries, from the Arteries into the Veines from the Veines into the heart againe.

In the heart there are two Ventricles or Concavities: the right and the left. The blood passes from the right Ventricle into the lungs by the Arterious Veine from the lungs by the Venous Artery into the left Ventricle of the heart and from the Left Ventricle into the great Artery and from thence into all the arteries from the body.

On the side of each ventricle there's a purse: which is called the eares of the heart, that on the right ventricle is made by the Vena Cava, that on the left ventricle by the Venous Artery: From these two Auricles the right and left Ventricle doe receive the blood which they expell out, the right ventricle into the lungs: the left ventricle into the great Artery.

The Arterious Veine arises from the right ventricle of the heart, it is improperly called a Veine because it hath a pulse, which none the lesse the Arteries have: The Venous Artery is improperly so called also: because it is a perfect veine, it having no pulse which all arteries have and it carrying blood from the lungs into the heart which none but the veines doe: and therefore also the Arterious Veine is an artery because it carries away the blood from the heart.

An artery is a white hard substance made up of many hard skins that it might be able to keepe in the blood which would otherwise force a passage; for if you cutt an artery, the blood will break out so forceably that you cannot possibly stop it. The blood of the arteries is of a fresher colour then that of the veines, the reason is this. The blood passes through the lungs immediately before it goes into the arteries, now it is strained through the lungs as through a sponge, and besides, the Aire the lungs draw within, so abates the heat of it and purges it from grosse vapours, that it makes it of a fresh colour, for heat makes it dark as you may see in bulls and in men that have a hott liver, and this purging of the blood is the principall end of its Circulation. Any arteries come from the great Artery, which rises from the left ventricle of the heart. A veine is a darker kind of substance made up of thinner membranes then the arteries: The veines doe all rise from the liver, from the Venae Cava and the Vena Portae and so are diverted into the whole bodie; the blood when it comes into the small veines from the arteries which are joyned to them in the extremities, goes into the liver and from them by the Venae Portae too, it sends its blood into the Vena Cava and from the Vena Cava it goes into the right auricle to the heart, and through the right auricle into the right ventricle and goes by the Arterious Veine into the lungs.

Finch had been very ill in Geneva on the way to Padua, and in a letter in 1653 to his sister he describes another illness. The treatment he received is perhaps worth noting; also the letter at the same time shows Baines' devotion to Finch:

I did some few dayes since never thinke to have beene able to have written you word of my health, for on Nov. 18-28 it pleas'd God to visitt me with the bitterest fitt of sicknesse that I ever underwent, I was sett upon by a Squinancy and its constant companion a Feavour which in me was more violent than ordinary, and a violent distillation, the second day after I fell sick I was not able to swallow I sent for Sybaticus and Molinettus the Physitians in Padoua and they pronounced me a dead man, (but it hath pleased God to bee mercifull to me) I was lett blood, used cupping glasses applied to my shoulders glisters (*sic*) and Purg... [*torn*] all within two dayes, when on a suddain they being all desperate it pleased God to afford me some abatement; though after Mollinett was of opinion I should miscarry then being brought to that weaknesse. After 5 dayes fasting that I could scarce discern anything: Mr Baines, God reward him, 3 whole nights satt up with me and indeed was the onely comfort I had in my disease by his care and vigilancy: To be short after 14 dayes sicknesse this day I have been able to goe down staires, so that I hope that I may now say that I am recovered, Lett me intreat thee my dearest to give thanks to the Lord for his Mercy vouchsafed me:...

Bargrave in his *Travells* (1654–5)[1] describes a visit to Padua, and when he mentions having met Finch and Baines he praises them highly. "Here I had the favour to be matriculated into the University and to be entertained by all the English Gentlemen with all imaginable Cortesie, specially by Mr John Finch and his Sociat Mr Baines, two remarkable Patterns for learning and Virtue."

Finch was made Pro-Rector and Syndic of the University in 1656, and the following passage from Tomasinus[2] relates the duties and privileges of that office:

When there is no Rector to be had, or when he who has been elected is forced to be away for more than a month, then a Vice-Rector or Pro-Rector, as well of the Doctors as of the Juriconsults, shall be elected by the University such as shall be worthy of the Rectorate. This honour often fell to the Gymnasium. He undertakes the duties of the Rector, and enjoys the same oath of jurisdiction as the Rector swears to, his eminence and privileges, with the exception indeed of the position of headship, and the exterior purple gown of the Rector. He wore a long gown of ample sleeves like the Rector's but black in colour, and under this exterior garment he wore red clothing. He received the gown with solemn ceremony in the Cathedral church and was led to his lodgings by a numerous company. The last

[1] *Rawlinson MSS.*, Bodleian Library, No. C. 799.
[2] *Gymnasium Patavinum Jacobi Phillipi Tomasini, episcopi Æmoniensis...Utini...*MDCLIV. "Concerning the Vicerector, Syndic and the Counsellors." Chap. xxiii (translation).

M.

Vice-Rector of the Masters of Arts was Dominus Samuel Geisufius, 1617, who died from a heavy fall from his horse.

From this time, since the office of the Gymnasium had lapsed, the Syndic, after a few years, was honoured by the title of Vice-Rector, with a large power of office. He indeed at the solemn functions of the University, that is to say, at the Disputations and the promotions of Doctors, wears a gown reaching down to his ankles, and thrown over it another long, sleeved gown of black silk, which the Bedell of the University takes charge of for a fee. Each University had its own Syndic, who as the head of the same does all those things, which formerly the Rector and the Vice-Rector undertook. The Counsellors attend on the Syndics, who are elected every year on the appointed day of Elections, in the beginning of the month of August in the presence of the most illustrious Rectors of the City, in the order and number given above. Should any Syndic, as well of the Juriconsults, as of the Masters of Arts, be absent, the Counsellors of each Germanic nation shall take his place.

Andrich[1] mentions that the Scottish nation had already given one Syndic —"Henricus Lindisy Scotus MDCXL-I"; while amongst those who followed Finch in the office were "Guilielmus Stokeham," "Emmanuel Timoni," "Richardus Collins." and "Thomas Tompson." Andrich[2] gives an account of Finch's election and of the important events during his tenure of office, and we learn that young Finch was well thought of by his contemporaries at Padua.

JOHN FINCH, ENGLISHMAN, 1656-7.

On the 1st of August 1656 Master John Finch, "having been elected without opposition, by the consent of all, and with great applause, remained *viva voce* Prorector and Syndic." On the 23rd of September the University senate, as Faciolati says, "ordered the Chancellors, that if anyone had obtained honours not by the consent of all the voters, but by the greater number only, commonly called 'by majority,' to declare this in the diploma, but they should give the diploma in a less decorated form, not on parchment but on paper." At the meeting on the 29th of September, there being present the Syndic and Counsellors, it was decreed that the registers [matriculae] should be given out to the students and the Counsellors of the nations should stand faith for each scholar. Wherefore from this year the Counsellors interceded for those who had matriculated [immatriculatio].

On the 7th November, when the Turks had been conquered, it was declared that a book in Latin or Italian should be written to congratulate the Venetian State, and on the 11th of December, that two scholars that had received honours from the Venetian college without payment, since they wished to be paid from the funds of the Gymnasium, should seek from the University that which by favour, but not by law, perhaps it was able to grant. There are two inscriptions dedicated to Finch in the Gymnasium. One in the entrance before the halls E and B with a wreath (stemmate) and monument; the other in hall A (the great hall) with a carved wreath in which he is described, by the decree of the Jurists of the University, as a most zealous defender and restorer of the privileges of the scholars.

Later a monument was also erected to the memory of another English Syndic, Dr William Stokeham[3]. Prof. Darwin, who published a valuable paper "On monuments to Cambridge men in Padua" (*Trans. of Camb. Antiquar. Soc.* 12th March, 1894), gives a plate of the sculptured monument with inscription to Finch in the Aula Magna. Finch's arms were Argent a chevron between three gryphons passant sable, but here there is a mullet(?) on the chevron,

---
[1] *Loc. cit.* B. Prorectores ac Syndici.   [2] *Loc. cit.* p. 14.
[3] Quoted by Ward (from Stowe's *Survey of London*) in section on Baines in *The Lives of the Professors of Gresham College*.

Monuments to Baines and Finch in the Aula Magna, Padua

(The present University buildings are on the site of a former "Albergo del Bue" and the University is commonly

and the gryphons are falsely blazoned rampant. One of the three small monuments (all alike) to Baines in the Aula Magna is depicted also. Baines' arms were "sable two bones crosswise argent" (Gwillim) but here, as Prof. Darwin pointed out, the bones are placed saltirewise and really the arms of Newton are represented. Dr Peile, late Master of Christ's College, very generously restored these monuments at his own expense. By the courtesy of the Cambridge Antiquarian Society we are enabled to reproduce Plate II.

Some years after this Dr Edward Browne (1642-1708), son of Sir Thomas Browne, came indirectly under the influence of Finch. Dr Norman Moore writes in his *Medicine in the British Isles*:

Browne went to Venice and then spent some weeks in Padua studying Anatomy. The dissection was admirably done by a demonstrator named Marchetti, who had been instructed by Sir John Finch "one who in Anatomy hath taken as much pains as most now living."

This was probably Domenico de Merchettis, son of the surgeon Pietro de Merchettis and one of the first Anatomists to inject the vessels. He noted (in 1652) movements of heart muscle and muscle of the intestine independent of connection with the brain[1].

A letter written in 1657 to Anne Conway describes how Finch and Baines took their degrees in the autumn of that year:

My dearest Dear,

You may imagine that I have scarce time enough to sett pen to paper that make use of Dr Baines his letter and beleive it my Dear my persuading him to bear me company in taking my degree of Doctor was the occasion of all this busenesse that hinders my present writing for this week onely wee were both made Doctors of Physick, and you have no reason to be angry at my silence for my taking my degree hath shortened my stay ten moneths which otherwise I must have spent at Monpellier to that Purpose: Here is my Lo: V Scudamores sonne who married Mrs Mary Bennett who desired to live with me at Padoua having at Paris wayted on you; but the expectation of my Lo: of Winchelsea whose comming I wondered not permitted me not the opportunity to secure the Mr Scudamore in his desires....

This letter is undated but the next one was written from "Padoua 3-13 December, 1657" and refers again to the taking of the degree. Finch evidently intended to go back to England; "for I tooke my degree of Doctor together with Mr Baines the deferring of which on either part till wee had left Padoua had kept me six moneths longer from thee my dear then I now shall be...."

In this second letter Finch speaks of two Bologna dogs, which he and Baines had sent to Anne Conway, and gives rules as to their care. Baines wrote previously of one of them as a "Bolognia masty dogge." The *Oxford Dictionary* gives "masty" as an old form for "mastiff," but it would be impossible for "ladyes" to hold a mastiff on their "laps." Besides a mastiff could not be an "exceedingly low" dog. So we must conclude that they were house dogs of some kind.

I hope by this time the Bologna Dog and Bitch are safely arrived, which Dr Baines and I sent you by Captain Haddock, Capt. of the *Hannibal* desiring you to give him 40

[1] Haeser, *Lehrbuch der Geschichte der Medizin*, Bd. II, S. 283 and 328.

shillings or £3 for their carriage, he having a speciall care of them. The Dog is called Julietto and the Bitch Vittoria.

1. Let them eat Flesh but in small Quantity; rather giving them bones to pick then much meat, and be sure let them not eat salt meat. If they are fed by more then one person they will eat too much and dye. They eat sweet Almonds or cakes if there be not too much sugar in them for that will fill them full of wormes. Bread sopped in the dish is good for them.

2. You must alwayes have a glasse-full of Distilled Water of Goats Rue, the Apothecaries call it *Aqua Gategae* or *Aqua Rutae Caprariae* of which you must once every week give them to drink Letting them that day have no other water that they may be sure to Drink of it; and if either of them are sik at any time Let them drink of that water before you let them tast any other.

3. When you order them to be washed, give youre mayds speciall charge that they wash not their heads for that will quickly destroy them; but if their heads are dirty at any time with a little bran let them be cleansed, the rest of their bodyes with a wash bole may be washed all over; but the seldomer they are washed the better: and scarce ever in Winter is best. In the Summer let the Mayds Flea them for they will be exceedingly troubled with Fleas. For being exceedingly low they will gather them all up in the house.

4. If they are troubled with extraordinary shaking of their heads insomuch that they scratch their Ears because they Itch and their Noses will be much stopped Then give them very little to Eat and take some Frankincense and hold their heads over the smoke of it, and they will doe well.

5. If that the Bitch be with Puppy at any time shee will certainly Dye if anybody during the nine weeks should chance to touch her with their Feet about the belly so that it were well to keep her in her basket that time, though in the Summer the basket must not bee so warme as now, but it were best when shee is proud to keep her from the Dog for one year at least, for it is likely shee may dye in breeding.

6. They were used here in Italy to lye in the bed; for they will cry at any time if they have occasion to goe down and are very cleanly; but it may be your Mayds lye two in a bed and there they are inconvenient.

7. The more they are made much of the merrier they will be, for the truth is here they are never out of the Ladyes laps or Arms or at least their presence. Let them by all means walk with you in the Garden for it will doe them good.

In no clearer way is the affection of Finch for his sister shown than in his letters in which he asks to have a picture of her sent to him whilst he was in Italy. Some of these passages also help to throw light upon the portrait of *Sir John Finch at his Studies* which at present hangs at Burley-on-the-Hill. He wrote from Padua on 1st November, 1652, very soon after his arrival there:

...Your Picture will be the most acceptable thing can come from England by a messenger, and I shall return you my owne for it if I can find any man that is eminent at drawing small pictures, but if I cannot heare of any, you cannot prize mine so much as I yours, and therefore I shall get nothing by the change....

And again, a few days later, he says: "...I make no doubt that Mr Frederick will find some means of conveying your picture to me, which I infinitely love to see...."

Anne Conway evidently had wished to have a portrait or miniature of her brother at this time, and he replies from Venice 10–20th February, 1652–3:

...I thanke you dearest for your affection in desiring my picture, I doe not thinke I shall find any able hand to draw it unlesse in Florence or Rome, if I can at Venice I will send it

Plate III

Sir John Finch at his Studies (portrait at Burley-on-the-Hill)
By S. Van Hoogstraaten

you, and the price will be your own picture in exchange which I shall covet more earnestly in regard I have none of you but what is in my heart. Your garter and hair are rêliques I enshrine as carefully as I can.

Finch had a miniature done of himself but it was not a great success and no trace of it can now be found. He had lost no time in having the picture done and writes from Venice 13th May, 1653:

...Dearest I had my picture done in little by the best hand I could hear of, but it was so much below my expectation that I was resolved not to send it, but had it been the best under Heaven I had been disappointed of a messenger. I shall not, I beleive (*sic*) have it done in little till I come to Florence or Rome....

The painting of John Finch at his studies (Plate III) has for many years been considered to have been done by a Dutch artist. Peter De Hooche had been suggested but authorities did not agree on this point. In 1915 Mr Lionel Cust told me that there was a "pendant" picture by S. Van Hoogstraaten (1627–1678) in the Royal Picture Gallery at the Hague of a woman (Frontispiece) standing with a letter or manuscript in her hand. As may be seen by comparing the two pictures, they are extraordinarily alike; both Finch and the lady in the other painting are represented as literary people; the same kind of dog is in the foreground of both pictures; a cat appears in both; the whole vestibule, pillars and glimpse of the Italian garden are very similar; and the background of both pictures is practically the same. Mr Cust writes[1] that the picture of Finch "is in itself remarkable both as a composition and for its admirable painting...."

It is unknown who the lady was, but is it not very natural to expect that there may be a very close relationship between the portraits? Certainly there can be no doubt that Van Hoogstraaten painted them both. He is known to have visited Italy and England, but unfortunately Finch never speaks of this picture of himself in the letters that are preserved. The lady in the picture at the Hague has an aquiline nose as the Finch family had in those days, and it seems very probable that Finch had his sister painted (from a likeness sent to him) in the same situation as himself, and the dogs which appear in the pictures may be those which he and Baines later sent to Anne Conway. This attempt to identify the lady is supported by a passage of a letter written by Finch from Padua 9–19th November, 1653, "...I heare no news of your picture though many Dutch from Flanders and Holland are lately come hither...." Unfortunately a careful enquiry has failed to reveal any record of a print or engraving representing Anne Viscountess Conway. Paintings by S. Van Hoogstraaten are rare and Waagen[2] knew of only one in England and that in the Bridgewater Gallery. It must remain an open question, for the present, as to when and where these companion pictures were painted.

[1] Lionel Cust and Archibald Malloch, "Portraits by Carlo Dolci and S. Van Hoogstraaten," *The Burlington Magazine*, no. CLXIII, vol. XXIX, October 1916.
[2] *Treasures of Art in Great Britain*, 1854–57, vol. II, p. 52.

CHAPTER IV

PISA

There is nothing in the Burley letters which would lead us to think that Finch and Baines returned to England before 1660. However in 1659 they had removed from Padua into Etruria, and Finch soon came under the notice of the Duke of Tuscany, for in this year Finch was appointed Professor of Anatomy at Pisa. He was the first and possibly the only Englishman to receive this honour.

It was a very important period at the University of Pisa and Finch was surrounded by distinguished men. Marcello Malpighi had come from Bologna in 1656, and for four years was in the chair of Theoretical Medicine[1], but it was not until the year 1661, after his return to Bologna, that he added another proof (if any further were necessary) of the truth of Harvey's conception of the circulation of the blood, when he watched through a microscope the blood coursing through the vessels on the surface of the lung and bladder of the frog. Borelli, the Physiologist and Physicist, was made Professor of Mathematics at Pisa in 1656, and Fabroni[2] relates how Malpighi supported Borelli in a controversy against Finch. "He [Borellus] received the patronage of Malpighius against John Finch, who obstinately denied that he was the first of all to have seen in tunny-fish, and sword-fish and other like fish that the optic nerve does not lie in the hairs, or threads collected into a bundle, as in men and quadrupeds, but in a certain complicated membrane." Borelli was the first to apply the laws of Physics to the problems of Physiology and his great work *De Motu Animalium* was published in the years 1680 and 1681.

In regard to Finch's appointment in the University of Pisa we must quote Fabroni[3] again at some length in order to obtain an idea of the intimate relationship which existed at that time between the Etruscan Court and the University. "Under the patronage of the Grand Duke and the peculiar care of his brother (Prince Leopold) the celebrated Accademia del Cimento, which preceded the Royal Society of London and the Academy of Sciences at Paris, was established at Florence in 1657[4]."

---

[1] Fabroni, *Historia Academicae Pisanae*, Pisis 1795, vol. III, p. 688. Medicinae tum Theoricae tum Practicae Ordinarii & Extraordinarii magistri—Marcellus Malpighius, Bonon.—1656–1659.
[2] *Loc. cit.* vol. III, p. 466.   [3] *Loc. cit.* vol. III, p. 533 (error in pagination for 532).
[4] *Diary and Correspondence of Dr Worthington*, edited by James Crossley, MDCCCXLVII, vol. I, p. 342 note.

This Academy has been described as "the greatest glory of Italy after Galileo." Emphasizing the truth of the first aphorism of Hippocrates, "experience is fallacious and judgment difficult," *provando e riprovando* was chosen as the motto of the Academy. I have seen a print of the *Accademia del Cimento* with a group of *virtuosi* seated about a table, some mathematical and physical instruments in the foreground and on the wall in the background the motto and the coat of arms, an oven with three crucibles or retorts upon it.

An account of the work performed by the Academy was published by the Secretary in 1667, and dedicated to the Grand Duke Ferdinand II; "with the favour of your Patronage, the encouraging invitation of your Mind, with the Honour of your Presence sometimes stooping to join us in the Academy, sometimes commanding us to your Royal Apartments, you have bestowed upon it an Immortal Glory." A translation of this book by Richard Waller, F.R.S., was published for the Royal Society in 1684 entitled *Essayes of Natural Experiments made in the Academie Del Cimento.*

Targioni Tozzetti[1] gives a list of the "famous anatomists" who were maintained and paid by the Grand Duke Ferdinand II of Tuscany and were favoured by his patronage: "Marcello Malpighi, Claudio Aubriet, Carlo Fracassati, Silvestro Bonfigliuoli, Nicolò Stenone, Giovanni Finckio, Lorenzo Bellini, and Tilmanno Truttwyn."

Fabroni writes:

Not for more than two years did the Academy use the works of Auberius, and afterwards for a year the chair of Anatomy was vacant, and in 1659, the place was given to John Finch a noble Briton with 450 hundred asses (centussium) in payment. The love of letters and the study of philosophy, which he had heard were in the house of the Princes of Medici especially cultivated, caused him to visit Etruria: in which he had scarcely set foot when he was plied with all honours. And whom shall we call happy, if not those, to use the words of Pliny, whose industry is proved, not by messengers and interpreters, but by the Grand Duke himself, and Leopold his brother, not only by their ears but also by their eyes? The love of knowledge acquired by some, to them was inborn and innate, whence it happened that they dwelt with learned men, like parents with their children. Nor would you have those things of little importance, which Finch used to put before their eyes. As an example, I will bring Berigard as a witness, who speaking of the chylus, says thus: "it is not carried by the mesaraic veins, as all antiquity believed, but by certain very minute veins which modern writers call milky, because on being cut they produce sweet milk. These being dispersed through the mesentery send out many branches to the intestines, to the pancreas, to the right jugular vein, and thence by ducts to the heart, which John Finch, a noble Englishman, Anatomical Ordinary in the Pisan Gymnasium, very clearly showed, as also many other things very worthy of account, before the most Serene Grand Duke, with no less praise and glory than William Harvey the pride of his renowned nation, of which he (Finch) may be called another hope, and perhaps, if it please God, he will show other ducts belonging to the breasts and uterus."

It is only just to state that Finch did not discover the lacteals, for they were described by Aselli in 1622.

[1] *Atti e Memorie inedite dell' Accademia del Cimento*...Firenze, MDCCLXXX, Tom. III, p. 192, § ccxliii.

We know also from Borellius[1] that Finch argued with many before the Grand Duke concerning the cramp-fish (torpedine) and attributed this much to it "that one who was troubled by a paralytic tremor had affirmed...that the touch of that fish had given his arm a grievous pain for two days." This person may be identified with Thomas Baines. At the beginning of a note-book in Sir John Finch's handwriting (dated Pisa 14th-24th January, 1663-4), "Cap. I. de Torpedinae tremola" is an account of the dissection of a torpedo-fish, also an amusing note, which is printed in vol. II of the *Finch Report*, 17th March, 1659–60, "the Grand Duke had sent them a live torpedo-fish, and (not knowing what sort of creature it was) they had taken it up in their hands, the result being a pricking sensation like that which comes when you suddenly put cold fingers to the fire. If the hand is not quickly taken away, the pain goes up the whole arm. Dr Baines, having very delicate nerves, was affected for some time afterwards, but Finch and Henry Brown [I think his clerk] were all right as soon as they removed their hand." It is of some interest to note that Baines always wrote in a shaky hand, and indeed his important letters to friends in England were generally written by another person and he merely signed them. Probably he was afflicted with paralysis agitans. Much later Finch writes to England, 3rd–13th January, 1679–80, that he still wishes students sent out to Constantinople to act as amanuenses especially for Baines "who is much incommoded as to the use of his hands in writing."

Finch never published an account of the torpedo-fish, but there is a paper in the *Phil. Trans. of the Roy. Soc.* LXIII, p. 461, "Anatomical Observations on the Torpedo," by John Hunter. Fabroni continues:

There were certain things concerning the optic nerves of another fish, about which Finch and Borellius were less agreed, which disagreement gave cause for that writing, which obtained a place amongst the posthumous works of Marcellus Malpighius. When Borellius wrote about these things in letters, Finch was absent from Etruria. For he had obtained leave from the Grand Duke to revisit Rome and Naples and the region with Thomas Penis [? for Baines], a Briton also, whom the similarity of studies had brought together, so that they had all things in common. He observed many things, and not a few related to natural history, that he might satisfy not only himself but his patrons. Not many months after he returned to his first employment dignified with title, as Adrian Van der Broechius witnesses, of physician to the Queen of England, which honour he received in the spring of 1665. The King increased it by committing to him the care of his affairs with the Grand Duke, as the "Resident." Nor did the liberality of the King end here. Ten years after he sent him as legate to the King of the Turks, and wherever he was he cultivated the learned friendship of the Medici Princes by all kinds of services, and the desire of investigating new things.

When he first came to Etruria he had with him an anatomical "sector" who seemed to be the most skilful of his times, called Tilman Tructwyn, of Ruremond in Flanders. You would have said his hands had eyes, and he believed nothing he had not seen. He also belonged to the hall and perhaps was of the academy of Pisa, and witnesses are not wanting who affirm that he died at Florence at the beginning of 1678, for a long time practising medicine after he had given up his work at the hospital of St Matthew.

[1] *De Mot. Animal.* part II, p. 441.

Targioni Tozzetti[1] gives an account of this man Tructwyn

> Il Tilmanno poi era un Anatomico trattenuto e stipendiato nella Corte del Granduca, ed in suo Manoscritto assai voluminoso che conservo nella mia Libraria, si chiama: *Tilmannus Tructwyn Rurae-Mundano-Sycamber, Medicinae Doctor, et Magni Etruriae Ducis ab Anatome.* Nella nostra Villa di Settignano era il suo Ritratto, impresso sul Gesso da formare, gettato sul Rame intagliato, e accomodato coll' inchiostro, come se si fosse dovuto tirare sulla Carta. Era rappresentato Giovine di bello aspetto e vivace, vestito allo Spagnuolo coll' Iscrizione:
>
> > Tilmannus sic ora gerit, sic pulchra inventae
> > Lumina; vis mentem cernere, scripta lege.
>
> Vi era altresi un Emblema, esprimente una Mano con Occhio nel suo dorso, la quale teneva fra il Pollice e l'Indice, un Coltello Anatomico, ed intorno vi era scritto:
>
> > Ecco l'occhiuta man, che quanto vede
> > Crede esser vero, e non quanto si dice.

What a splendid picture this gives of the trained Anatomist, who apparently could see with his hands, so acute had his sense of touch become! This figure was used in the XIX century only with the eye at the end of the finger.

Tozzetti[2] had in his possession an original MS. written by Tructwyn of *Observations on Medicine and Pharmacology.* On the first page, following an epigram in Latin to the naturalist Francesco Redi and a short preface on the nobility of Medicine, Tructwyn wrote an apology for setting down his own epitaph and gives the epitaph itself. He did not die until about ten years later.

> ......Ne de Sepulcro sollicitus haeres esset, neve vivorum neglentia obesset mortuo, Humanitatis suae memor, hocce Epitaphium Dialogicum sibi vivus posuit:
>
> > A. 1669 die 1. Ianuarii.
> > Quis iacet hic? Nullus. Quis saxo hoc clauditur? Omnis.
> > Clarius ista, rogo, dic, age, vera Lapis.
> > Tilmannus parva situs est Trutwynius urna
> > Qui sibi Nullus erat, omnibus Omnis erat.

In Finch's note-book, "1670–71, March 19–29, Easter Day Florence," he is referred to again as "Tilmann Trewijn, Anatomist of Ruremond." A young man, Robert Clifford, son of Sir Thomas, died very suddenly, and Trewijn (or Tructwyn) performed the post mortem. Finch gives an account in Latin of the autopsy. The young fellow before he died confessed to Finch himself, seeing that there was no Anglican Chaplain to act as confessor, and as John Finch was dismayed at Sir Bernard Gascoigne's suggestion that one of the Irish fathers from the Convent of the Benedictines be called in. The confession is given in cypher.

This account has taken us rapidly over the eventful periods which Finch and Baines spent in England before the former was appointed Ambassador to

---

[1] *Atti e Memorie inedite dell' Accademia del Cimento e Notizie Aneddote dei Progressi delle Scienze in Toscana*, Firenze, MDCCLXXX, Tom. I, p. 275, §XCVI.

[2] *Ibid.* Tom. III, p. 350.

Florence. That Finch was made physician to the Queen of England is quite true, for in 1662 there was issued a "passport for Sir John Finch physician to the Queen Consort, and Dr Thomas Baines to go to Florence[1]." Fabroni in his list of the "Anatom Magistri[2]," gives "Jo Finchius Brittanus 1659–1663," but Finch spent from 1660 to 1662 in England. His successor was "Carolus Fracassatius, Bononicus 1665–1668," who was a friend of Malpighi and who carried out experiments on infusion[3] in animals. It would appear that the chair of Anatomy was unoccupied from 1663 to 1665.

In Florence Finch was associated with another famous scientist, Nicolaus Steno (1631–1686), the Danish naturalist. Steno came to Italy in 1666, was Professor of Anatomy in Padua, and then in Florence was physician to the household of the Grand Duke Ferdinand of Tuscany[4]. "He (Stenonius) in the Hospital of St Mary Nova in Florence together with Finch and Laurence Lorenzinus, gave evidence of singular industry and acumen in enquiring into things, which were said to be either not then understood or not well understood[5]."

We give the following epigrams on "Dr John Finch" as an Anatomist, in both Latin and English. Targioni Tozzetti[6] considered that they were written "in the hand of the famous Valerio Chimentelli." They were very kindly copied for me from the MS.[7] in the Biblioteca Magliabechiana Nazionale in Florence. It is of interest to note that Finch's work on the lymph ducts is referred to, that the heart is spoken of as "the fount of life," and that the venous blood is very picturesquely described as "wearied when its work is done."

In the second epigram the writer contrasts the macrocosm and the microcosm, and pictures the steady progress of civilization from the East to the West. The results of Medical Science on the other hand, he rightly understands, will help to lengthen men's days, and the sunset of life will be more and more distant.

Ad Excellentissimum D. Joannem Finchium Anglum Anatomicae artis Professorem Celeberrimum.

Clarus ab avulsis toto venis orbe Britannis
Ultima iam studii sic quoque meta tui.
Mente argus, cultro lynx, docto daedalus ore,
Cuncta secas, cernis cuncta nihilque taces.
Vena riget, seu fibra regat, vel ductibus erret,
Seu quid deliteat viscere, vase, sinu.
Qua nova depreensum scandens fert semita succum
Migret ut in rorem candida gutta rubrum.

---

[1] *Calendar of State Papers—Domestic*, 1661-1662, p. 513, Oct. 12th.   [2] *Loc. cit.* vol. III, p. 687.

[3] In apoplectics he injected various substances into the blood stream in the vain hope of dissolving the coagulated blood in the brain. He also did work on transfusion.

[4] *Encycl. Brit.* 11th ed.   [5] Fabroni, *loc. cit.* vol. III, p. 538.   [6] *Loc. cit.* Tom. III, p. 193.

[7] Codice già VII, 600; oggi II. IV, 282, a carte 101. Biblioteca Magliabechiana Nazionale, Firenze. I have to thank Mr C. Hagberg Wright, Superintendent of the London Library, for writing and having these epigrams transcribed for me.

Qua ruit hic fartim vitali e fonte resultans,
Qua redit esacto lassus ab officio.
Nempe hominem nunc findere scite, ac fingere primum
Divinae monstras nil minus artis opus.

Aliud.

Scindit Iber pelagum audaci dum puppe repostum,
Grandis in Occasum, grandior Orbis eat.
Abdita tu Parvi retegens penetralia mundi
Flectat ab occasu longius, ipse facis.

Aliud.

Finchius en radiat sectrici victor in arte.
Caprigeni pulcher pellem sic findit Apollo.

To the most Excellent Sir John Finch, Englishman, the famous Professor of Anatomy.

[You come] full of fame from the British, who are divided from the whole world, so also is now the last aim of your study. Keen in mind, a lynx with the knife, clever with a learned tongue, you cut everything, you see everything, and you are silent about nothing. Whether a vein irrigates, a fibre controls, whether something wanders through the ducts or lies hid in some organ, vessel, or sinus, [you tell] how the sap of the body is caught and carried upward by a new path, so that a clear drop changes into red dew, how this gushes forth in a thick stream from the fount of life; how it returns wearied, when its work is done. Indeed you show that to cut man up with skill is no less a work of divine art than to make him in the beginning.

Another poem.

While the Spaniard cleaves the remote ocean with audacious prow, let the great world, and the greater, move towards the sunset, you by disclosing the inner secrets of the little world, cause it to swerve further from its sunset.

One more.

Lo! Finch shines victor in the anatomizing art. Thus beauteous Apollo splits the skin of the goat-born [*i.e.* flays Marsyas the satyr].

Finch did not confine his attention to Anatomy but was always much interested in chemistry and pharmacology.

If there was anything that pleased their (patrons') minds, it was the investigation of nature, and no one came to that hall and had exercised in it to whom singular honours and rewards had not been attributed. To these belonged John Finch, who prided himself that he had discovered certain new things about salts, and had explained his method of extracting them from herbs; all indeed praised his industry but they also gave commendation to Oliva because he had before shown all these things before the eyes of many, of which Charles Fracassatius bears witness, and adds this, "the beloved Oliva made a Polypeiram ac robustam Encyclopaediam" of the Etruscan hall[1].

The world has not greatly changed and even now-a-days we find discoveries have been made before, and the credit has to be given to the "Olivas"!

Finch had a curious mind, and in those of his note-books which were at Burley-on-the-Hill there are notes in his handwriting dealing with a large variety

---

[1] Fabroni, *loc. cit.* vol. III, p. 615.

of subjects. For the most part these notes do not record any original work by Finch, but consist of extracts from various writers. A few of the headings are "Diamonds and pearls"; "The Caribee Islands"; "Experiments made of the sympathetic powder by Sir Gilbert Talbot," no doubt the "powder of sympathy" of Sir Kenelm Digby; "Murano glass-works"; "The Wind"; "A Treatise of Astronomy, wherein is discoursed of the Flux and Reflux of the Sea" (many extracts about this), etc.

Finch was also very credulous and was ready to believe supernatural wonders. He wrote at great length to his sister in 1656–7 about some images and pictures in a Greek Church in Smyrna, which "come down of their own accord on St George's day, if the priest do not take them down, and go out of the church." Another extract in his note-book is about a supposed rain of wheat[1]. In this letter Finch also writes "At Jeball, 300 miles from Tripoli, is a whole province where, by petrifying blast or sand, all things are turned into stone in the same postures they had when living. I have a piece of a camel's bone thence, and have ordered a body of man, woman or child to be brought me. The Duke of Florence has a hen with all her chickens in stone, and all the colours of their feathers. One in Venice has a bough with apples on it, all the natural colours." There are numerous notes on the making of saltpetre and on the history of gunpowder, but I have been unable to see any reference to the extraction of salts from herbs.

Tozzetti in his book on the Accademia del Cimento[2] already referred to, and under the heading "Experiments on the Digestion of some Animals," quotes the following from the minutes or journal of the society: "15th May 1659. Twelve fowls sent to the house of the English Anatomists, a sack of sifted millet and more coops to keep them in properly, etc." Tozzetti adds "these Anatomists very probably were Giovanni Finchio and Tommaso Forbes of whom I have treated at length in volume 1, page 272." Like Harvey, many Anatomists and Physiologists, even down to the present day, have been so enthusiastic in their experimental work that they have turned part of their homes into a laboratory in order that observations and experiments might be carried out at all times of the day and night.

It is unfortunate that in their letters neither Finch nor Baines speaks of this work. The following passage from a book[3] on the Accademia del Cimento, if it is not an account presented to that Society by them, at any rate we must conclude that it presents the results of the experiments of these two "English Anatomists."

[1] *Cal. of State Papers—Domestic*, 1656-1657, p. 287.
[2] *Atti e Memorie inedite dell' Accademia del Cimento*, Tom. II, part II, p. 599.
[3] *Essayes of Natural Experiments made in the Academie Del Cimento....*Englished by Richard Waller, Fellow of the Royal Society, London, 1684, p. 150.

Experiments about the Digestion of some Animals.

Wonderful is the Force wherewith the *Digestion* of the *Hen*, and *Duck* kind is performed for they being crammed with little Balls of Solid *Crystal*, were dissected by us in a few *hours*, and opening their *ventricles* in the *Sun*, they seemed to us covered all over with a glittering *Coat*, which examining with a Microscope, we found it to be onely strewed over with exquisitely fine and impalpable powder of *Crystal*.

In others likewise, crammed with hollow Bubbles of *Crystal-Glass* with a small hole in them, we were amazed to find of the said *Bubbles* some already broken, and powdered; others onely crack'd, and filled with a *whitish* Substance, like curdled *Milk*, got in at the small hole; and we also observed, that those were bettered *powdered* (than the others) which had in the *Maws* with them a greater *Quantity* of small Stones. And 'tis less strange, that they break, and grind to *pieces*, *Corke*, and any hard *Woods*, as *Cypress*, and *Beech*, and rub to Powder *Olive-stones*, the hardest *Pine-apple* Kernels, and *Pistaches* put down their Mouths, with the Husk on. *Pistol bullets* in Twenty four Hours we have found much *Battered*: and several little hollow square Boxes of *Tin* were observed to be some *scratched*, and battered, others tore open from one side to the other.

CHAPTER V

ENGLAND

Finch and Baines—their names are coupled as easily as David and Jonathan—returned to England after the Restoration late in the year 1660 or early in 1661 and were well received by their countrymen.

Soon after their arrival in England Baines was chosen Professor of Music at Gresham College as successor to Dr Petty, and Ward[1] gives the date as 8th of March, 1660 (? 1661). We find a letter from Finch to his brother-in-law Lord Conway, dated 2nd February, 1661, in which he writes that there was an election for a fellowship at Gresham College and that he wished his Lordship had appeared for Dr Baines[2]. There is no evidence to show that Baines was specially qualified to hold a musical professorship.

"The Doctors," as their friends were fond of calling them, were together made Fellows extraordinary of the Royal College of Physicians, "1660–1 Martii j. Admittantur jam Socii Extraordinarii Dr Joannes Finch et Dr Baines," as the Roll Call has it. But at that time the number of Fellows was already complete and the register shows that this action by the College was not to be taken as a precedent. Finch was connected with Harvey by the marriage of Heneage Finch to Harvey's niece. Finch and Baines were elected partly on account of the great benefits Harvey had conferred on the College[3].

1660–1. Februarii XXVI. Ob praeclara Doctoris Harvei, nobis nunquam sine honore nominandi, ejusque fratris germani Eliabi, in Collegium merita, placuit Sociis omnibus praesentibus (praeterquam quatuor) Doctorem Joannem Finch et Doctorem Thomam Baines (Patavii doctorali laureâ ornatos), adaucto tantundem, in eorum gratiam, Sociorum numero, in Collegium, seu Socios Extraordinarios, adsciscere: eâ tamen lege ac conditione, ne res haec facile in exemplum trahatur.

In 1663 a new charter was granted to the College and the number of Fellows was increased to forty. Finch and Baines were enrolled as Fellows with the same privileges enjoyed by the Fellows who were admitted under the old charter.

On the 10th June, 1661, John Finch was knighted by the King, but Baines did not have this honour conferred upon him until some years later. Wood[4]

---

[1] *Lives of the Gresham Professors*, London, MDCCXL, p. 228.
[2] *Calendar of State Papers—Domestic—Charles II*, vol. xxx, p. 501.
[3] Munk's *Roll Call of the Roy. Coll. of Physicians*, 2nd ed. vol. I, p. 299.
[4] *Loc. cit.* p. 228.

Plate IV

Sir John Finch

From portrait at Burley-on-the-Hill (see p. 51)

tells us that "giving a visit to Edw. E. of Clarendon L. Chancellor, he (Finch) was by him conducted to his Majesty; and being by him presented as a rarity, his Majesty no sooner saw, but instantly confer'd upon him the honour of knighthood as a Person who abroad had in a high degree honoured his Country." Charles II's active interest in science and especially in Anatomy may be recalled (*vide* Pepys, 16th January, 1669). The present Master of Christ's College, Dr A. E. Shipley, *The Cambridge History of English Literature* (vol. VIII, p. 358), in his section on "The Progress of Science," points out that Charles II's taste for science may be explained by his ancestry on his mother's side—the Medici.

Dr Worthington[1] writes to his friend S. Hartlib in 1661: "...By the newsbook I perceive Dr John Finch (the Lady Conway's brother) is knighted by the King. He was Dr More's pupil, and one of excellent improvements when at Christ College; and he hath gained much reputation abroad. He is furnished with all things convenient for the making experiments in the way of physick by the Duke of Florence."

On the 20th June, 1661, Finch and Baines received the degree of Doctor of Physic from the University of Cambridge, but conferred on them *in absentia*, in virtue of their years of study at Padua and of the medical degree granted to them by that university[2].

Cum vir eximie nobilis Johannes Finch, eques auratus et Pisae, magni ducis Hetruriae, professor publicus, et dignissimus etiam vir Thomas Baynes, duodecim abhinc annis admissi fuerint apud nos Cantabrigienses ad gradum magisterii in artibus et postea in exteras regiones profecti, diuque apud Patavinos commorati, non sine summorum applausu, et Anglicani nominis honore gradum doctoratûs in medicina ibidem adepti sint; in patriam demum reversis superiori anno iisdem gratia concessa est, ut hic a ud nos admitterentur ad eundem gradum, statum et honorem, quibus apud Patavinos prius insigniti fuerant. At vero cum ipsimet in personis propriis ob importuna negotia, quibus impliciti et detenti sunt adesse non possint; Placet itaque vobis ut vir nobilis Johannes Finch admissionem suam recipiat ad dictum gradum sub persona Doctoris Carr in medicinâ doctoris;—et Thomas Baynes suam itidem sub persona Johannis Gostlin inceptoris in medicina; et ut eorum stet eisdem pro completis gradu et forma.

Both Finch and Baines were interested in the formation of the Royal Society and their names appear together, "John Finch," "Tho. Baines," amongst the "signatures of the persons who, on the 5th of December, 1660, resolved to form a society for promoting experimental philosophy[3]." However the Charter of Incorporation did not pass the Great Seal till the 15th of July, 1662, and the second Charter on the 22nd of April, 1663, in which the officers were practically all renominated and provision was made that all persons whom the President and Council should receive into the Society within two months from the date

[1] *Diary and Correspondence of Dr Worthington*, vol. I, p. 339.
[2] Munk's *Roll Call of the Roy. Coll. of Physicians*, 2nd ed. vol. I, p. 299.
[3] *The Signatures in the First Journal-Book and The Charter Book of the Royal Society*, Oxford University Press, in which the signatures are reproduced as photogravures of the originals.

of the Charter should be named Fellows, and on the 20th May, 1663, "Finch Sir John Kt." and "Bayne Thomas M.D. afterwards Kt." were admitted as members and therefore as Fellows[1]. Amongst other names enrolled at this time were those of Elias Ashmole, John Evelyn, Kenelm Digby, Wm. Petty, George Duke of Buckingham, George Bate, M.D., William Croome, M.D., John Dryden, and Christopher Wren, etc. Finch and Baines both attended the meetings of the Society whilst they remained in England, and on 15th May they were "with several others nominated a committee for a library at Gresham College and for examining of the generation of insects[2]."

By the courtesy of the Royal Society I have been allowed to look over some unpublished letters from H. Oldenburgh (the Secretary) "to Sir John Finch at Florence," written in the years 1664–1669. They are four in number. Oldenburgh hoped that Finch would soon have his *History of Poysons* ready, and tried to arrange that Finch might send a letter from time to time telling of the advance of knowledge in Italy, as Finch was well known to Prince Leopold and to other "virtuosi" in Florence, Naples and Rome. Oldenburgh tells of recent papers that had been read before the Royal Society. Finch evidently did not answer this first letter and the second repeats the same request. The second letter brought an answer from Finch which was read on "assembly day," and the Royal Society wished to thank him for conveying a history of the institution to the Grand Duke of Tuscany. In the fourth letter Oldenburgh wished to have a copy made of a "Greek MS. on Chymistry in the Florence Library," and wrote that the expenses of such work would be borne by Sir Robert Moray and himself.

In the Burley papers very little light is thrown upon the life of Finch and Baines during their years of residence in England. Sir John Finch's house was in Kensington and indeed it now forms part of Kensington Palace. Here they may have lived together, but it would seem from letters to the Conways that they stayed with Heneage Finch at the Inner Temple. Baines also had lodgings at Gresham College. They attended meetings of the Royal Society, enjoying the friendship of some of the distinguished men of the time, and paid occasional visits to the Conways at Ragley.

There is a very interesting series of letters in the Burley MSS. from Heneage Finch, afterwards Lord Chancellor, to his young son Daniel at Oxford, and in these Finch and Baines are occasionally mentioned. "If you return in convenient time (*i.e.* from Bath to Oxford), 'tis likely that Dr Baynes will give you a visit before he leave England[3]." Heneage Finch apparently did not take Baines altogether seriously in his endeavours to give advice to young Daniel,

---
[1] *The Record of the Royal Society*, 3rd ed. 1912, pp. 15–16.
[2] *Journals of the Roy. Soc.* vol. I, p. 18.   [3] *Loc. cit.* p. 208. 1662, Aug. 7th.

Plate V

From portrait at Burley-on-the-Hill (see p. 51)

although the father himself was constantly urging his son to study and to avoid frivolity. However Daniel was a diligent student and a model son, which makes one wonder the more what was the nature of Baines' advice. Heneage Finch writes: "Dr Baynes hath written you a large treatise of good counsell in his own phrase, which though I know you do not want, yet I would have you take kindly when you see him, for he that intends a respect to you must always find himself respected agayn[1]." In the same letter, Heneage Finch says: "Your uncle and Dr Baynes are still at Tunbridge." Later we shall see that "the Doctors," and especially Baines, had much to do with the education of Daniel.

A note-book of Finch's contains items of scientific subjects under discussion with "S. Allen" and "T.B." (*i.e.* Baines) at Rusthall in August, 1662. "Rusthall" evidently refers to the place of that name near Tunbridge Wells, as in that same month they stayed at Tunbridge.

Finch and Baines were never married, but we have Finch's word for it that he was in love at this time. However this love affair came to nought and the reasons he gave for not marrying are most amusing and show Finch to be a most cautious but really very simple young man. Heneage Finch wrote to Conway on 22nd June, 1661:

I am heartily glad that love has at last obtained such power over my brother Sir John Finch, as to fix him in England, when he thought himself bound in gratitude to the Duke of Florence to run away from the favours of the English Court[2].

Finch writes to Lord Conway, 27th July, 1661, describing the tour of small places which he and Baines were making, and adds:

So soon as we came to Chester I found my Lord Masarin (*sic*) bewayling the narrow missing of your Lordship. Wee dined together but during dinner his Lordship, congratulating me my designs in Warwickshire, and mentioning the person, made Dr Baines astounded that the intelligence of such an affair had so soon crossed the sea, when it arrived his notice so late...from Chester we went to Shrewsbury, then to Ludlow, Hereford, Gloster, Bristol and Bathe, whence I went by coach to London, but I sent Con to Ragley with the Horses... I have at large discoursed with my Brother concerning my amours, who after he had at first told me, he would never be against the thing I liked, told me there were many circumstances little advisable: in so much that T.B. triumphed in his judgment. The Dr having added one scruple more, which was that in case I had children and dyed: how was it evident shee would not dispose of her estate to her second husband's children or person. Thus my Lord what I scrupled for another score: I find my Brother very cold in upon the Account of Reason in point of Treaty: so that tis well I have not necessitated myselfe at present to a further discourse and noyse.

Baines seems to have been just a little selfish in the matter of Finch's intended marriage. Some years later Heneage Finch was again hoping that

---
[1] *Loc. cit.* p. 212. 1662, Aug. 23rd, and also *Calendar of State Papers—Domestic*, 1661-1662, p. 463. "1662 Aug. 18th Tues....to [Lord Conway]...The Doctors are both at Tunbridge and are going to Italy."
[2] *Calendar of State Papers—Domestic*, 1661-1662.

John Finch would marry, and wrote to him in Italy: "all your friends are well and my Lord Conway still in towne. Wee meet often ourselves with wishing you here, and contriving preferments for you, one of which, you may be sure, is a good wife[1]." It is never suggested that Baines was ever in love with anybody but Finch, and had the latter married, Baines would have been utterly disconsolate, so wrapped up were they in each other.

There are a large number of letters (145) from Henry More to Anne Conway in the British Museum and he often mentions Finch and Baines. In the autumn of 1661 they visited Grantham where More was born, for there are notes in Finch's commonplace book of conversations there on various medical questions. More writes that he had "also mett with Sr John Finch and Dr Baines at Grantham, that they promised me to call at Cambridge at their return out of the country[2]." In another letter in 1662, More says:

> Sr John and Dr Baines gave us the happiness of their good society here at last, with much ado we detained them 4 or five days. They stay'd in Holland beyond what I could imagine. But not for nothing for Sr John has raysed his revenue near 250 pound more then it was before. They go into Italy before next Summer. I was urging Sr John as forcibly as I could not to go at all. But what thay will do, God alone knows, scarce the Great Duke[3].

It was probably during this stay in Holland that Finch heard of a blind man who was able by touch alone to distinguish colours. Sir John with characteristic zeal investigated this strange story and communicated the results of his experiments to his friend Robert Boyle, and the latter in his book on Colours[4] gives a splendid account of the whole proceedings.

> ...I'l here set down a Memorable particular that chanc'd to come to my Knowledge, since I writ a good part of this *Essay*; and it is this. Meeting casually the other Day with the deservedly Famous (since for his eminent Qualities and Loyalty Grac'd by his Majesty, with the Honour of Knighthood) Dr *J. Finch*, Extraordinary *Anatomist* to that Great Patron of the *Virtuosi*, the now Great Duke of *Toscany*, and enquiring of this Ingenious Person, what might be the Chief Rarity he had seen in his late return out of *Italy* into *England*, he told me, it was a man at Maestricht in the Low-Countrys, who at certain times can discern and *distinguish Colours by the Touch* with his Fingers. You'l easily Conclude, that this is farr more strange, than what I propos'd but as *not impossible*;...Wherefore I confess, I propos'd divers Scruples, and particularly whether the Doctor had taken care to bind a Napkin or Hankerchief over his Eyes so carefully, as to be sure he could make no use of his sight, though he had but Counterfeited the want of it, to which I added divers other Questions, to satisfie my Self, whether there were any Likelihood of Collusion of other Tricks. But I found that the Judicious Doctor having gone farr out of his way, purposely to satisfie Himself and his Learned Prince about this Wonder, had been very Watchfull and Circumspect

---

[1] *Finch Report* (Hist. MSS. Comm.), vol. 1, p. 456.
[2] Brit. Mus. *Addit. MSS.* 23216, f. 76, 16th Nov. 1661.
[3] *Ibid.* f. 86, 4th Jan. 1662.
[4] Hon. Robert Boyle, F.R.S. *Experiments and Considerations touching colours...The Beginning of an Experimental History of Colours*, p. 42, London, MDCLXIV, in 8°. The earlier Latin edition in 8° was printed in 1663.

to keep *Himselfe* from being Impos'd upon. And that he might not through any mistake in point of Memory mis-inform *Me*, he did me the Favour at my Request, to look out the Notes he had written for his Own and his Princes Information, the summ of which Memorials, as far as we shall mention them here, was this, That the Doctor having been inform'd at *Utrecht*, that there Lived one at some Miles distance from *Maestricht*, who could distinguish Colours by the Touch, when he came to the last nam'd Town, he sent a Messenger for him, and having Examin'd him, was told upon Enquiry these Particulars:

That the Man's name was *John Vermaasen*, at that time about 33 years of Age; that when he was but two years Old, he had the Small Pox, which rendered him absolutely Blind; that at this present he is an *Organist*, and serves that Office in a publick Quire.

That the Doctor discoursing with him over Night, the Blind man affirm'd, that he could distinguish Colours by the Touch, but that he could not do it, unless he were Fasting; Any quantity of Drink taking from him that Exquisitness of Touch which is requisite to so Nice a Sensation.

That hereupon the Doctor provided against the next Morning seven pieces of Ribbon, of these seven Colours, Black, White, Red, Blew, Green, Yellow, and Gray, but as for *mingled* Colours, this *Vermaasen* would not undertake to discern them, though if offer'd, he would tell that they were *Mix'd*....That all the difference was more or less Asperity, for says he (I give you the Doctor's own words) Black feels as if you were feeling Needles points, or some harsh Sand, and Red feels very Smooth....

To these Informations the Obliging Doctor was pleas'd to add the welcome present of three of those very pieces of Ribbon, whose Colours in his presence the Blind man had distinguished, pronouncing the one Gray, the other Red, and the third Green, which I keep by me as Rarities, and the rather, because he fear'd the rest were miscarry'd.

The following letter was written by Finch from Holland and addressed to his patron Prince Leopold of Tuscany. Unfortunately it is undated. It must have been sent whilst Finch was on this same trip to Holland, for the blind man is referred to and further details are given of experiments. This letter appears in a book published in Florence in 1773 under the title *Lettere inedite di Uomini Illustri, Per servire d' appendice all' Opera intitolata, Vitae Italorum Doctrina Excellentium*, a copy of which is to be found in Bodley's Library. The discussion on the preparation of anatomical subjects is of some interest.

To the Prince Leopold[1].

The lateness of this justly due hommage might cause us to lose the Most gracious favour of Your Most Serene Highness were it not that what may have seemed our neglect is itself our excuse. Because it was nothing but our very profound reverence (regard), which kept us from writing until now, anything worthy of Y.M.S.His notice. For, when we arrived at Rotterdam, for the purpose of visiting Signor Bilzio[2], famous for his anatomical discoveries,— we found that many were dying of the plague in that city, and what was more important to us, that Sig. Bilzio himself was in bed, with very high fever and lived in the very street in which the plague was raging most severely. All this however did not avail to check our curiosity, as we have obtained some pamphlets from the said Bilzio, and been in his house

[1] "The three following letters were written by John Finch, not so much in his own name, as in that of his travelling companion and greatest friend Thomas Baines. Finch was a member of a noble English family, and was very greatly esteemed and beloved by Ferdinand II, and Prince Leopold. He was appointed by them Lecturer, at Pisa, in Anatomy, in which science he was most proficient. He resigned the Lectureship in May, 1665, having been appointed by his Sovereign, Resident at the Court of the said Grand Duke "—note in the Italian.

[2] Evidently Louis De Bilsius (or Bils), whose supposed methods of preserving bodies and of dissecting without loss of blood, caused such a stir in the 17th century. The States of Brabant are said to have bought his secrets.

while he was confined to bed. We could not give Y.M.S.H. an account of our observations previous to carrying out our quarantine, which noways diminishes our devotion and loyalty to Y.M.S.H., whose commands we honour even when far distant.

The forty days of quarantine being now expired, I shall give Y.M.S.H. particular notes of our observations on the three matters referred to in my last. Sig. Bilzio claims to possess the art of preserving dead bodies with the same colour as when they were alive; it is certainly true that he succeeds in preserving them complete, and inodorous, extracting from them only the bowels. Three corpses he has prepared, and he maintains, and others believe, that all the blood vessels and entrails are preserved in such a manner that they may be used for anatomical purposes in summer, as well as in winter. But only small portions of the entrails, and a few badly prepared blood vessels, are really to be found. All the same, these bodies have caused a great talk, although the muscles are so shrivelled up that because of their smallness, they can scarcely be recognized as such, and even then some of the number are missing. The States General have conferred on Sig. Bilzio the favour of being permitted to charge one reale [one franc], from every person desirous of seeing these bodies.

Sig. Bilzio claims to have the secret of *cutting bodies* without loss of blood but demands a very large amount for divulging it. On my return I shall bring with me a pamphlet printed by him in which he states that he will not disclose the said secret unless on payment of the sum he requires: that he makes use of it daily; and that by means of it he is able to attain a perfect knowledge of the lymphatic and lacteous vessels, which however, I do not believe; what I know for certain is, that this way of preserving bodies was proposed and practised by Paré, long before Bilzio. This man does not understand Latin or any other language but French and Flemish. He never had any teacher of anatomy, but has a remarkable aptitude for dissection, to aid him in which he used in France to steal at night, the bodies of executed criminals which remained on the gallows. For the rest he is a person of no learning, and unable to explain himself, for which reason he excuses himself from giving reasons. I have no faith in one who boasts without good grounds; I know however that if his bodies are worth paying a reale by each one who wishes to see them, our own *Tavole*[1] [probably anatomical plates]—a matter of greater importance—should suffice to make a fortune in Holland.

With regard to the blind man who distinguishes colours by touch,—we spent many days at Mastricht, in talks, and in making experiments with him; and really it is marvellous to see this man know by touch a pack of cards, play at piquet, and count so exactly, that it is impossible to deceive him. We observed, however, that at the commencement, he turned and re-turned the cards two or three times, before he could or would play—and we therefore suspected, that he might know the cards by some indication other than the colour; all the more, that he declined to name any card taken from another pack of new cards. On this account on the following day we invited him to our room alone, and Mr Baines commenced by changing the order of three cards, placing the knave of hearts in the room of the knave of clubs and so with the other cards; and then gave into his hand, this new pack. After turning them over and over, three or four times, he commenced to play, but always mistook these three cards, naming them in the order in which they are usually placed, and not discovering the trick that their places had been changed. Whence it is evident that he knows the cards by some other indication than that of colour; and it is wonderful that by his marks, invisible to us, he should succeed in recognizing cards he had known months and years before. I tried him with the cards daily. I am bringing both the pairs [? packs], in order that Y.M.S.H. may see that they have no marks. This blind man, however, cannot distinguish cards if they have been very much pressed, and are consequently very smooth and polished. As to colours he recognizes them easily by touch, if the stuff he handles be not extra fine, or very coarse and of various tints. I have with me five different colours of a striped stuff, accurately identified by him, very many times (especially in the morning when fasting,—

---

[1] See p. 7 and also Appendix.

because, after drinking, even a little, the sense of touch is less delicate), and he does this with such certainty that he taught us how to distinguish colours by touch, and I have written down the differences of them, according to his idea, which I shall bring with me along with the striped stuff, when I return. This affair may help to confirm our theory about colours.

As regards the Waters of Spa, we were astonished to behold some four or five hundred ladies and gentlemen who appeared in the best of health. These waters are a means of bringing together many, who would not otherwise easily have an opportunity of meeting. Whence from these waters, love, many's the time, springs anew. All the same, we consider them the best we have hitherto experimented upon, among the acid waters. They have a strong tincture of steel, or rather are strongly impregnated therewith, and we are of opinion that they are bound to have great efficacy in curing obstructions, purifying the breath, and strengthening the stomach, on which account they must be of special benefit in cases of dropsy, as also of headaches. There are four springs of different strengths, among which one is so strong as to cause vomiting in many people, although for some years back, its strength has been diminishing. We have drunk the water of all these springs, up to seventy ounces of the strongest; and therewith, I most humbly make my reverence to Your Most Serene Highness.

Your M.S. Highness'
Most humble, devoted, and obliged Servant,
JOHN FINCH.

We can readily understand that it is now rather difficult to follow the movements of the devoted pair, as they wrote few letters except to the Conways and no doubt some of them are lost. Finch's cousin, the Earl of Winchilsea, Ambassador at Constantinople, constantly complains bitterly in his letters that he has not received word from either of them. Finch and Baines were rather poor correspondents, it seems, but there was some excuse for Baines on account of the tremor in his hand. This very close friendship of Finch and Baines was cultivated at the expense of other associations.

Lord Winchilsea writes to Henry Browne at "Lighorne":

1662-3 Feb. 16 Pera. That my cousin Finch and Dr Baines were again heard of and proceeded on their journey towards Italy as far as Lions was strange noveltie to mee. I thought they were out of the world, and resolved wholly to forget their friends, that their friends might as justly forget them. For since my departure out of England, now two years and a half agoe, I have not received one line or syllable from them either in answer to my letters, I am assured were delivered to them, nor in correspondence to some tokens and demonstrations of my affection I made to Dr Baines, which neither beneath his acceptance nor his acknowledgement. I shall not write to congratulate their arrival in Italy, but if they at last think me deserving of a letter, I will answer it: but pray advise them, that it will be no sollecisme or breach of punctualitie is (*sic*) used in Italy if I take as much time to return answere to their letters as allready they have taken to answer mine.

However the miscreants later relented and Winchilsea forgave them both, but not without some show of sarcasm and humour, and writes to Finch[1], "yet if you intend to have a plenary indulgence and pardon, you must perform the

---

[1] *Finch Report* (Hist. MSS. Comm.), vol. I, p. 247.

penance of a pilgrimage to Constantinople," and to Baines he says[1], "I do wish not only for my sake but also for your owne that you would see Constantinople before going into England." Many times Winchilsea urges Finch and Baines to visit him in Turkey. Later on in the same year (8th April, 1663) Winchilsea writes to Finch "I send you herewith a character (cypher) that we may write the more freely to each other."

Winchilsea, for some years afterwards, especially when Finch became Ambassador in Florence, kept up a constant correspondence with Finch and writes often about curious things, and makes medical enquiries. On 25th May, 1663, writing from Pera, he prays for "a ball to try the goodness of water" and some "antidotes of poison."

[1] *Loc. cit.* vol. I, p. 247; same date, 30th March, 1663.

CHAPTER VI

LIFE IN FLORENCE

In 1661 Finch and Baines had sought the consent of the College of Physicians to go into Italy but had not availed themselves of that permission. Ward[1] quotes the following minute which appears in the register, "Sept. 30th 1661 Dominus Johannes Finch et doctor Baines summa cum urbanitate veniam abeundi in Italiam a domino praeside petierunt, obtinueruntque."

Sir John Finch and Dr Baines started out from England this time on 25th October, 1662. In the *Calendar of State Papers*, 1662, 12th October, there is an interesting entry giving Baines permission to leave Gresham College.

The King to the Lord Mayor of the City of London, and the masters, warders, and assistants of the Mercers' Company. Gives license to Dr Thos. Baines, Fellow of that College, to go and remain beyond his nine years, and requests that he may receive meanwhile all the profits of his fellowship, any statutes to the contrary notwithstanding.

They landed at Calais on 30th October. A few days later they met Alderman Backwell, who came to receive "the money Dunkirk was sold for" and which, Finch tells us, arrived in "forty-six carts." On this occasion the friends remained in Italy for about two and a half years, Finch presumably working at his Anatomy and in the hospitals, whilst Baines seems to have been of a much more retiring disposition and devoted his time to study. There are few letters of this period to friends in England and usually these record that certain gifts of "choisest Lucca oil," a "Parmesan cheese" or "Florence mushrooms" have been sent off.

In a letter[2] preserved in the Library of Christ's College from Anne Conway to Henry More, dated 5th December, 1662, occurs the following passage. We

[1] *Loc. cit.* p. 229.
[2] A number of letters from Anne Conway to Henry More were in the possession of the antiquarian James Crossley of Manchester, whose library was sold after his death in 1885 and 1886. I learnt from an old catalogue of the sale that this particular parcel of letters was sold for 9s. to "Tattersall." A letter of enquiry to E. Somerville Tattersall, Esquire, Knightsbridge, brought me a reply that he had sent my note on to J. F. Tattersall, Esquire, of Lewes, Sussex. The latter answered me that he had bought the letters in 1885, and by his kindness I was enabled to trace their further travels. Mr Tattersall disposed of two to a gentleman at Hastings, and these, being of interest to the Society of Friends, were presented to them, and are now in their Reference Library, in Bishopsgate Street, where I was allowed to see them. The other letters were given by Mr Tattersall to the Dean of Wells and he in turn informed me that he had presented them to Christ's College. Mr Norman McLean of Christ's has kindly transcribed for me passages from these letters which have any bearing on Finch and Baines.

see that even Sir John Finch's sister thought she had cause of complaint about his neglect of letter-writing and that of Baines.

I hear my Brother and Dr Baines are returned againe for Italy, I wonder you makes no mention of them, because you staied so long in London, where methinks they should have made you frequent visitts and have acquainted you with their intentions, I hear so little from themselves, it makes me very desirous to gitt what information I can from others, and therefore I hope you will pardon my desire to know what you have found by them, relating to their designes, if there be any thing of that kind which you have forgot to Impart to
      Dear Sir
       Your ever most entirely affectionate friend
          and humble Servant A. Conway.

Sir John was in high favour with the Grand Duke of Tuscany, and Thomas Baines writes to Lord Conway that one of the Duke's own coaches had been assigned to them[1], and in the same note he says that both he and Finch are failing in health. This was in August, 1663, and in October "the Doctors" were preparing for the trip to Rome and Naples already mentioned (p. 24). In the middle of October Finch writes that the Grand Duke is very kind and that he will send them to Rome in one of his litters[2]. Prince Leopold, the Duke's brother, gave them a letter of introduction to one Michel Angelo Ricci[3], "*Hujus itineris gratia has litteras dedit Leopoldus Princeps ad Michaelum Angelum Riccium XVII. Kal. Octbr. 1663.*"

Viene a cotesta volta il Sig. Gio. Finchio Cavaliere Inglese per passare a Napoli, ed intanto osservare costì quel che vi fusse di curioso, che non fusse stato da lui veduto l' altra volta che fu in Roma, e conoscere i più insigni per virtù. Questo Signore è molto amato, e stimato dal Sereniss. Granduca, e da me, per la sua virtù, come forse per la medesima sarà anche ben noto a VS. e si diletta grandemente della Filosofia, ricercando con curiosità non ordinaria le cose naturali, e la verità di esse. Viene in sua compagnia il Sig. Dott. Tommaso Penis (*sic*), ancor egli ripiena di virtù, e suo amicissimo: e perchè desiderano d' avere qualche introduzione appresso persona che sappia indirizzargli acciò possino sodisfare al loro virtuoso genio; e sapendo io che il mezzo di VS. può sommamente essergli favorevole, mi piglio sicurta d' inviargli a Lei, con fiducia che essi sieno per riconoscere nel medesimo tempo la di Lei singolare cortesia, e la parzialità del mio affetto, che anche in ciò bramo di dimostrargli, Prego però VS. a voler somministrare a detti Signori quelle notizie, che li bisognano, e si accerti pure di fare a me cosa gratissima; mentre resto ec.

This letter of introduction the two travellers evidently presented, for Sir John jotted down notes of this trip and quotes the opinions of Angelus Ricci on various subjects. These are in a note-book which is amongst the papers at Burley-on-the-Hill, and the dates are "Roma 24th Oct. 1663" and "Neapoli Nov. 14th." This Ricci was probably Cardinal Michel Angelo Ricci who wrote *Exercitatio geometrica de maximis et minimis*, London, 1668, which was published as part of a quarto volume together with a treatise by Mercator.

[1] *Calendar of State Papers—Domestic*, 1663, Aug. 3 (?), p. 226.
[2] *Ibid.* 15th Oct. 1663, p. 302.   [3] Fabroni, *loc. cit.*

The two following letters[1] from Sir John Finch to Prince Leopold describe some events on this trip to Naples and Rome. Finch's interest in snakes has already been noted. One of his note-books contains a list of the books contained in the library of M. Aurelio Severino, which he and Baines purchased.

To the Prince Leopold.

Having arrived from Naples on Wednesday evening, by the Grace of God in good health, we had decided to return to Pisa, without making a stay—and had ordered the horses for Monday morning; but having waited on Sig. Michel Angelo Ricci this evening, in order to deliver to him the letter which Your Most Serene Highness so kindly wrote him in our favour, we have been so charmed by his conversation, and most distinguished manners, that we very humbly beg to be excused, if we remain three days more in Rome, so as to enjoy for this short time, so important an acquaintance.

At Naples we had very detailed particulars of Sig. Tommaso Cornelio, a Mathematician and Physician of great reputation and friend of Sig. Michel Angelo Ricci: he has written a book entitled *Progymnasmata Physica* which was printed at Venice, and one part of which is dedicated to Sig. D. Alfonso Borelli[2]. He is a follower of Descartes and a great favourer of things new, and on this account is hated in Naples by those who swear loyalty to their old teachers. In his book he says that before *Pecquetto*[3] or any other he was the inventor of the hypothesis of compressing of the air by elastic force. He is a Calabrian by birth a lively acute man, and like most of his compatriots very hot tempered.

It would surpass the limits of a letter were I to give Y.M.S.H. particulars of all we have done about the natural phenomena of Naples. We have gone through some adventures, as for instance on our second visit to Mount Vesuvius, when after wandering twelve miles on foot, notwithstanding many guides, we did not succeed in arriving at the top of the crater. Then as regards sulphurous earths, we made collections of very beautiful flowers of sulphur: of extremely fine sal ammoniac, of mineral alum, of super-fine nitre, not inferior to that of the ancients: but seeing such a variety of substances in that scorching ground which is hollow below, as one perceives from the booming sound made by every stone cast upon it, we took a bell-shaped alembic, and collecting the smoke from the most fiery spots, to see if oil of sulphur would result, we extracted a phial-full of liquid, which though not acid, like artificial oil of sulphur, produces nevertheless some effects proper to it—such as discolouring metals with its smoke, etc. All these collections, along with that part of the library of M. Aurelio Severino which we purchased from the Secretary of the Kingdom, we have dispatched to Leghorn, in order that the Most Serene Grand Duke and Y.M.S.H. may satisfy your curiosity.

We also got information as to the way in which manna is collected, and we have sent various kinds of it.

We thought it our duty to give Y.M.S.H. this short note of our journey. To-morrow morning, we have to go to the Marchese Patrizi—proprietor of the *Grotto di Serpenti* (the Serpents' cave)—to be informed by him about the place, and how we should proceed.

Would God we could demonstrate by our doings the extreme desire we have to serve Y.S.H. in all Your Commands—of which, the more Y.M.S.H. deigns to lay upon us, the more we are favoured, who in all sincerity of heart full of humility and respect, count it an honour to be recognized by the whole world for the most reverent admirers of Y.M.S.H.; and wishing the Most Serene Grand Duke, and the Most Serene House every happiness that Heaven can bestow: we remain

From Rome 24 November, 1663. GIOVANNI FINCHIO.

[1] *Lettere di Uomini Illustri*, Florence, 1773.

[2] "This part is only a Latin letter, feigned by Cornelio to have been written by his deceased friend, Marco Aurelio Severino Crettigena"—note in the Italian.

[3] The brilliant Jean Pecquet, who discovered the receptaculum chyli and thoracic duct, whilst still a student. He prescribed "eau-de-vie" for all ills, but for himself it became an "eau de mort" (Bayle).

M.

To the Prince Leopold.

I return most humble thanks to Y.M.S.H. for the most gracious letter delivered to me by Sig. Michel Angelo Ricci, the evening before my departure from Rome. On Sunday I arrived at Pisa, having first visited on the journey the Grotto di Serpenti belonging to Marchese Patrizi at the Sasso, to which courteous and most kind nobleman I am particularly obliged.

I entered the cave by myself, which in breadth could only hold a man lying on the ground and in its greatest height does not attain four feet. I waited for the serpents issuing forth, but saw none. The people of the place told me that they only came out in the warm spring weather; and the major domo of the Marchese said that as many as 65 had been seen round the naked body of a diseased man. The sick dose themselves with opium, so as not to be frightened and move, and so scare the serpents; and it is said that they, after being licked by the serpents, come out cured of any skin disease.

These serpents are not poisonous, that is clear from the chance that happened to a certain person who boldly went in naked without taking opium. Unable to bear a serpent on his flesh, he squeezed it hard with the calf of his leg and was bitten by it. He, however, fled for two miles without stopping, with the blood flowing from him, but was otherwise none the worse. A man of mean condition who went in alone, after taking opium, was found dead in the cave, but this they put down to the excessive dose of opium taken by him, and not to the harmfulness of the serpents.

The cave is so hot that although the door (which is closed with bars when a patient goes in) remained open, it made me sweat: on which account I am inclined to believe that those few who are cured—if indeed there are any—are healed by the action of the Hypocaust, or dry-stove heat, which is advantageous in diseases of the skin.

It is certainly true that there are many serpents in that cave, because although I did not see any, I noticed a number of holes where they live, and I collected several of their sloughs which I have brought with me, to see if similar skins are found elsewhere. The inhabitants, to distinguish them from other serpents, say that these have a white line all round the neck.

I have no other notes to give Y.M.S.H. about this journey. I beg Y.M.S.H. to excuse me for wearying you, and kneeling at your feet (on behalf also of Sig. Tommaso) with the profound respect which our sincere devotion to your person requires and commands, and wishing to Y.M.S.H. increase of glory, and victories, and the highest happiness to all the most Serene House; I remain

GIOVANNI FINCHIO.

The 10th day of December, 1663.

In December, 1663, Finch reassumed his work as Lecturer in Anatomy in Pisa, and Targioni Tozzetti[1] quotes a letter of "Pietro Andriano Vanden Brocche" [*Epistolae*, page 51]: "Finchius iam Titulo Medici Reginae Britanniae honestatus, ante paucissimas dies ad Professionem Anatomes Pisis rediit. Octavo Kal. Februarias in Theatro Anatomico, suum in Cadavere Humano munus auspicabitur. Incisio a Tilmanno fiet."

Sir John Finch turned his friendship with the Grand Duke to good account by obtaining a position for one of his cousins, Colonel Charles Finch. The Earl of Winchilsea in writing to this brother about the matter says: "I have not been un-busy to try to find you some employment worthy of yourself and your

---

[1] *Atti e Memorie inedite dell' Accademia del Cimento*...Firenze, MDCCLXXX, Tom. I, p. 273.

family, and am glad to hear from Sir John Finch that, by his favour with the Archduke he has obtained for you the command of a regiment in Italy[1]."

Finch and Baines came back to England some time in the year 1664, but the exact date is uncertain as they have left little record of their movements. Henry More had the pernicious habit of omitting to add the year when dating his letters to Anne Conway, but it seems most probable that the letters, from which the following extracts are taken, were written in 1664. Finch and Baines had become such old cronies in Italy that perhaps their ways appeared a little queer to their friends in England.

More finds these "Italians" past understanding and again they come in for a measure of blame in the matter of their correspondence. Interesting light is shed on Baines' philosophy; he did not blindly follow the traditions of his old tutor. More writes (Brit. Mus. *Addit. MSS.* 23216, f. xx, 212):

> I had the happiness of enjoying Sr John Finch his company severall times at London, to whom I gave also a copy of my book. He tells me he will read it over very considerately at Florence and does not seem so confident of contrary conceptions as he did heretofore. Dr Baines has solicited his invention to try all tricks possible to evade the force of my reasons, but I have not found him successfull yett. I asked Sir Johns opinion of the Letter of Resolution, because I perceived your Ladyship had a minde to know it. He told me the Authour had writt ingeniously but not so fully that severall other things might be added that would make to the same purpose. That was the summe of his Answer. I gave Mr Solicitor [Heneage Finch] also one of my Books. Sr John told me he was resolved to read it over, and I think himself sayd as much to me. And it may not be unlikely if he finde it worth the whyle, for he has a fitt Genius for such things, as I discerned by that little converse I had with him. And Tully was an excellent Philosopher as well as a famous Advocate and Oratour. I had the other day two or three hours discourse with Crellius his son and find that the want of Philosophy is most certainly the ground of the Socinians gross mistakes in those grand points of our Relligion. But the man was a pretty man, and of a fair and honest Temper, so farr as I can discerne. But they are...[*word illegible*] in that low corporeall dispensation of T.B. [Baines] that can phancy nothing but matter, and are but Aristoteleans in Philosophy, or nothing at all. I mean, are for his system of the World, and understand not the laws of matter nor the Systeme of Des Cartes, whose philosophy is the best Engine I can give against such erroneous fabricks in Relligion. Theres nothing more occurs to my mind for the present....

In 1671 and 1672 More published his *Enchiridion Metaphysicum* in which he reveals a change of view in regard to Descartes' philosophy, and this fact seems to show that this letter was written before these years.

And again on 29th August (*ibid.* f. 242) More says:

> Sr John promised me frequent letters too, and that Philosophicall one, but I do not expect it, he is the best company that can be present but the least when he is absent. If there were none wiser than myself, I would not have him to go into Italy, but stay and write his letters here. I am not certain that Dr Baines Palsy was so sensibly encreased upon him, I beeleevve it is some time more, sometime less, but methought he looked rather better than he used to doe. The Socinians are free though in all conscience, and a little too bold in some respects, but their Genius is too strait and short for some thinges. But what I told you is most certain

---

[1] *Finch Report* (Hist. MSS. Comm.), vol. 1, p. 308, "Pera 26th April 1664."

that their great mistake in Divinity, is from their incapacity of conceiving any thing but Body or Matter....

On 14th Sept. the Platonist writes (*ibid.* f. 246):

The Italians are not yett come to Cambridge. I left a very extraordinary kinde letter at Sr Heneage Finches for Dr Baines to be given him when he returned to London, and wrote also as civilly as I could, to Sr John Finch to invite them to Cambridge, but I have received no letter from either of them. I understand nothing of the Italian Genius....

In March, 1665, Finch was appointed to be King Charles II's Resident at Florence, at the court of the Grand Duke of Tuscany. Sir John insisted that Baines must go with him to Italy. It is sometimes said that Baines acted as Physician to the Embassy, but he is not mentioned as such in the letters. It has been stated that Baines was knighted on this occasion, but in the *Calendar of State Papers* I find him first mentioned as "Sir Thomas" on 12th May, 1673. Baines could not have spent much of his time at his work as Professor of Music, and on the occasion of this departure, Sir Andrew Clark agreed to provide a reader in his place at Gresham College. Finch also made the necessary arrangements for leaving England and sold his house (now Kensington Palace) to his brother Heneage, who, in turn, left it to his son Daniel, second Earl of Nottingham, and in 1689, Nottingham House, as it was then called, was purchased by King William III.

Pepys in his *Diary* writes of riding out to Kensington and "...going into Sir H. Finche's garden and seeing the fountayne, and singing there with the ladies, and a mighty cool place it is, with a great laver of water in the middle and the bravest place for musique I ever heard."

Anthony Wood[1] thus describes Finch's arrival in Italy:

Upon his arrival at Florence, Sir Bernard Gascoigne (a known friend to the English nation) did with an undeniable Civility press him to take quarter at his own House, till he should be farther provided: which he accordingly accepted, and the Duke was pleased to employ the said Sir Bernard to his Majesty's Resident, with such notices and respects as he found then convenient. In the end all things being agreed upon, as to the manner and dignity of his Reception, the said Resident made entry in a very noble Coach, being attended with an answerable train, in rich Liveries, and a great number of other Coaches, beside the whole Factory of Leghorn, who very kindly appeared in a handsom equipage to do him all possible honour. Thus attended he went to the Palace, and received Audience first from the Great Duke, and two days after from the Dutchess and Prince, acquiting himself with a singular grace throughout the whole Ceremony.

This was an important appointment for Sir John Finch, but his contemporaries did not think him unworthy of the honour. The Earl of Winchilsea writes to Heneage Finch[2]:

Yours of the 9th March I received the 21st of June, and cannot but congratulate the honour his Majestie hath donne my cousin John, whose meritts having mett with such an

---

[1] *Loc. cit.* vol. II, Fasti p. 59.   [2] *Loc. cit.* vol. I, p. 379. June 25th, 1665.

employment, hath now an opportunity of shewing the world those abilities he is master off and honouring our family as much abroad as you do att home.

It is rather remarkable that in the year 1666 three members of the Finch family should be occupying such important positions; Heneage was Solicitor General at that time, his brother was Ambassador at Florence, and their cousin Heneage, fifth Earl of Winchilsea, was King Charles' representative at the Porte. Finch's usefulness at Florence to the English Government is well set forth in two letters of the Earl of Arlington, then Secretary of State, to the Earl of Winchilsea:

...and I may with truth say I have had the good luck of late to have given my hand to the establishing your cousin, Sir John Finch, in an employment in Italy, which I hope will not only bee to his Majestie's advantage and his own satisfaction, but your Excellencie's also, in finding such a hand in the midway through which wee may correspond better in the future[1].

And again:

I hope your Excellencie having Sir John Finch for your correspondent soe much nearer than we are and the means of sending to you, you will not have cause to complain of the want of knowing all our news[2].

Winchilsea made other use of Finch than in diplomatic matters, as we have noted before, and used to send money to his agents in Leghorn in order that Sir John might "purchase pictures, statues and medals."

There was no important political crisis during Finch's term of office at Florence and most of his official correspondence deals with very minor trade disputes and such-like. However he seems to have done this kind of work well, and the MSS. preserved at the Bodleian Library[3] reveal how punctilious he was in the preparation of his speeches to the Grand Duke and of his reports on apparently very trifling matters.

Some extracts from these MSS. may be of some interest, as they throw light upon certain trade disputes. The other documents are concerned with certain matters described at much greater length in cypher letters of Sir John Finch to his brother-in-law Viscount Conway which I have summarized (*vide infra*).

MS. Rawl. A. 478, *fo.* 1.

[Heading] "Extract of a letter of Sr J. Finch. March 8. 16$\frac{68}{69}$."

Suggests that for some grievances, not named, "the Duke of Florence pay for them by Ounces by a severe Treaty," and he "must stoop, or else the trade of Florence silks is lost and Florence and Legorne ruined."

Continues about Algiers, and English Mediterranean shipping. Algerians have seized English ships, which are much too small and have no guns, but are loaded with rich commodities. Suggests burning some of their (Algerians) ships in port, which would diminish

---

[1] *Loc. cit.* vol. 1, p. 369. April 20th, 1665.   [2] *Loc. cit.* vol. 1, p. 395. Sept. 13th, 1665.
[3] *Rawl. MSS.* A. 477, pp. 100, 129–131; A. 478, pp. 1, 120, 132.

their strength and scare them. Afterwards when peace was made, only ships of force to be sent out, to go out from England, and return to England or Holland, not to stay in Mediterranean as a constant temptation to the Barbary coast. These larger ships would also act as Convoy ships, and receive money from smaller ships. At present English ships went under Genoese Convoy ships.

At the end of this letter is this note in the same hand:
The answer to this of the 26. March 1669. I have offered your last proposition to his Majesty and R. Highnesse who approue your invention in it but cannot yet conclude it practicable.

MS. Rawl. A. 478, ff. 120–142ᵛ.

Copy in Italian and English of a letter from Sir J. Finch to the Grand Duke of Tuscany, representing English grievances. Dated Florence, Mar. 21. 1671. Very long.

Includes in this one memorial, what was in his other memorials of Nov. 2. and Feb. 4.

1. Asks that woollen manufactures and other merchandise from His Majesty's Kingdoms or Plantations to Legorn with Bills of Health, may be freely brought on shore without being sent to the Lazaretto to make Quarantena. 1stly: because English Factors lost the benefit of the market for their sale. 2ndly: charges of Lazaretto heavy. 3rdly: the opening of their goods in the Lazaretto predjudicial to them. Goods from France, Venice, etc., not thus exposed. 4thly: not done in former times.

2. Second demand is that all woollen manufactures made in the Dominions of his Majesty may be freely sold throughout the whole State of His Highness, paying only same duty as was paid before the prohibition of their sale throughout the whole state.

3. Third demand. All Consolati (or Consolages) are made by Captains and Mariners either to obtain averages upon the goods they carry in consideration of dammages they pretend to have happened to their ships; or to be freed from paying a penalty to the Merchants for not consigning their goods in good condition. He demands that English captains be not permitted to make "Consolati," but that they shall be left to the English maritime laws, the Tribunals being exorbitant and unfair.

4. Fourth demand that all English slaves in Algiers or elsewhere, that shall be ransomed and brought to Legorn, shall be putt into perfect liberty; and not be subject to imprisonment or sequester, or be summoned before Tribunals for any pretensions that they have not paid their ransom. Refers to the case of Armiger.

5. That the number of guards upon ships be reduced. That the Public Health was preserved when only one guard was allotted to one ship, and is still sufficient in other neighbouring ports.

Thanks him for his assurances of strict orders for keeping the Custom-house books of Legorn in giorno: also for remedying abuses in weighing at the Public Stadera, and for allowing him to use his Tribunals for abbreviating lawsuits. Does not question but he will grant these demands also.

In the autumn of 1665 Daniel Finch, son of Heneage, was sent out to Italy to further his education. In the Burley papers there are many letters from his parents and brother to the studious young man. Finch and Baines acted as Daniel's guardians, and the latter evidently was the lad's tutor and was able to give him much of that advice at which the father had smiled! We learn from these letters in what high esteem both medical men were held. "Your letter from Florence puts an end to our doubts caused by that from Venice, you being now in such good hands as my uncle and Dr Baines[1]." To the son[2]: "I have written to your uncle to desire him to settle the rates you are to pay for living there, which is absolutely necessary to bee done and of which he is the truest judge, nor can I suffer you to live at his charge...When any occasion shall draw you to see any other part of Italy, if Dr Baines can bee prevayled with to protect you with his company and advice in your journey you are happy. But bee sure you beare the whole expense of so much time." And Elizabeth, Lady Finch (daughter of Dr William Harvey's younger brother Daniel), writes when she learns that her son has reached Florence, "my mind is at rest." Father to son, 7–17th December, 1666, "I know the care and kindness of Dr Baynes, and desire to return him my hearty thanks[3]."

In a letter to Sir Heneage Finch, the Earl of Winchilsea wishes that his son also could go out to Italy in order that he might take advantage of all that such a trip would offer to a young man, and that Finch and "the Doctor" might "overlook him for a few months." Winchilsea's opinion of Sir John could scarcely be higher:

...for I noe (*sic*) no gentleman either in England or out of it soe capable to doe great things in the breeding of my son as he, and he is of such honour and worth and soe experimented in the world that if I were to advise the king for a Gouvenour of a Prince of Wales (when it shall please God to bless him with one) I should prefer my cousin your brother[4].

This is the greatest praise, even if due allowance be made for the manner of expressing it in those very polite days.

Several times I have come across short "songs" and poems in the notebooks or commonplace books of Sir John Finch. Some of the verses were "designed for my dear Lady Conway, now in heaven," as he described them in one of the books. One of the "songs" begins with the line "All Pow'rfull God! whom nought can Disobey," and another "Thou bad Enquirer of the Birth of Ill![5]" Finch must have been in a very sad mood indeed when he wrote the following poem and seems to have taken a morbid pleasure in his sorrows. Was it written after the voluntary close to his love affair?

> Build me my Mansion in a Cypresse Grove
> Hallow'd by Dirges of the Turtle Dove,
> Where the Wood Echoes out the Nightly howl
> Of Hungry Wolves, and the Shrill Screeching Owl,
> Where the Pale Shadows of the Silent Night
> By their Glidings Mortalls doe affright,
> Where that the closeweav'd Boughs forbid each Ray
> And sable Shades blott out the cheerful Day,

---

[1] *Loc. cit.* vol. I, p. 403. Nov. 29th, 1665.   [2] *Loc. cit.* vol. I, p. 403. Nov. 30th, 1665, O.S.
[3] *Loc. cit.* vol. I, p. 445.   [4] *Loc. cit.* vol. I, p. 423.
[5] Also referred to in *Calendar of State Papers—Domestic*, 1668–1669, p. 659.

> Where awful Flashes of the Blackened Sky
> Through Trees more dark their Clearings multiply.
> And Thunders from the Hills redoubled make
> The unshorne Cliffes with Men and Beasts to quake
> Amidst some Craggy Rocks, whose aged Heads
> From their Amazing Heights doe Roaring Shed
> Large Streames; whose chafing murmurs as they goe
> Fill with confusion all the Plaines below.
> Hang me my Room with Black, and as in Urnes
> Let there some dully shining Taper burn.
> Whilst that the Glimmering light which faintly streames
> Spreads Universall Sadnesse with its Beames.
> Blest Solitude free from all Eyes and Ears,
> From busy noise, fond mirth, vain Hopes and Tears.
> Bury'd alive in this forgotten Cell
> Where Horrour Cares and wretched I doe dwell.
> Here will I sitt and sigh and weeping Sing,
> Banish all Joys but what my Tears doe bring.
> Till that my Drooping soul with Woes opprest,
> On the soft mossy Floor finds Peaceful Rest.

There can be little doubt that Henry More referred to this poem in the following letter written to Anne Conway from "C.C.C." (Christ's College, Cambridge), 23rd March, 1666-7[1], but the verses are not to be found with More's letters.

...I quite forgott to send you Sr John Finch's verses, but I knowe not whether my forgettfulness in this point or my mindfulness were the more tolerable. They are a very melancholy copy of verses and it is in obedience to your Ladishipp's commands more than my allowance of my own judgment that makes me send them. I have sent you the originall, but keep a copy of them myselfe, as an ingenious monument of Sr John his Melancholy. There is that of a poetical character in them, but your Ladishipp is so well fortifyd with the sacred principles of Christianity and Philosophy that you'll easily remember that your brother's mournful muse is but like a melancholy fitt of musick, reaches only the passions, offers nothing of reason why we should be sad. Whatever though of Theologicall or Philosophicall difficulty insinuated in the verses, I knowe your Ladishipp will easily solve, which makes me rest the more satisfyed with my adventure of sending them. They talke of hopes of peace, I pray God send it. Your Ladishipp will not do well to lett Mrs Foxcroft read those verses without this Antidote. The Referees of her husband's case have, or will, report to the King, that they have concluded as most fitt that Sr Edward Winter and her son be sent for hither into England, but that Mr Foxcroft keepe his place there where he is. This Dr Whichcoate told me this day, for very good news. I was with her son Ezekiel and communicated her postscript to him....

Dr Whichcote was one of the group of Cambridge Platonists.

Mrs Foxcroft was apparently an almost constant visitor at Ragley: she was Elizabeth, daughter of Christopher Whichcote and niece of Dr Whichcote. Her sister Mary married John Worthington (1618–1671), Master of Jesus College and a friend of More, who presented the latter to the living of Ingoldsby in 1667. Worthington's *Diary and Correspondence* was edited by the late James Crossley of Manchester.

[1] Brit. Mus. *Addit. MSS.* 23216, p. 90.

Sir Edward Winter (1622–1686) was agent at Fort George (Madras) and in the *Dictionary of National Biography* an account is given of his quarrel with George Foxcroft who was sent out to succeed him. Winter brought up a charge of treason against Foxcroft on a slight pretext and had him and also Foxcroft's son arrested, and claimed the place of agent again. This happened in the autumn of 1665, but the news did not reach London till early in the year 1666–7. Winter had friends in court but it was not until April, 1667, that Charles II signed an order to Winter to surrender the fort, and it was only when six armed vessels appeared before the fort of Madras in May, 1681, that the order was finally obeyed.

In the spring of 1667 Baines went with his protégé Daniel on a trip to Rome and Naples. Thus Finch, for practically the first time since they had met, was separated from his bosom companion and in his solitude writes from Livorno on Sunday "Aprill 15–25th" to his "Dearest Dear" a long and very characteristic letter. This goes a long way to reveal his thoughts on friendship and is an apologetic for those men who feel that they can have but few close friends.

> When I most seriously consider what is that most endears to us the thing which we call life: I am, I professe extreamly at a losse to rayse the esteem and Value wee sett upon it. For if I am to speak as a Christian the enjoying this World is the renouncing of it; mortifycation and self denyal being the badges of them who have anything else to entitle them to Christianity besides theyr Baptisme: and I apprehend this reluctancy so essentiall a point in taking up the Cross, that if any by the Melancholy of their Temper were carry'd on the same practises with delight which I with much naturall Aversion found myselfe to undertake: I cannot apprehend that what is Height of Christianity in mee, would amount to common Morality in them. Actions of Religion and Morality receiving their Determinations from the inner Principle they flow from: and not from any externall appearances, which are either good, indifferent, or bad according to the intention that gave them being: If I speake as a Philosopher, there is nothing that renders our life more to be valued then (*sic*) that of Brutes but Discourse with each other and the result of that friendship wee make from a similitude in our Sentiments and Inclinations and Religion from which the Philosopher is by no means to be excluded.
>
> As to Discourse there so few Persons who know how to discourse and so few of them brought to our knowledg and acquaintance with whom wee desire a Discourse: and of them so many yet fewer wee desire to have friendship with that I thinke what our Grandfather Sir Moyle Finch told our father when hee said hee had spent £80 upon a supper for his friends at Cambridge: that he who had more years and experience could gett all his friends at a little round table in his study which held not above six Persons: might be applied to all Mankind for I should much question how that he who has numerous friendships had none at all, so then this Great World that considered in Generall is of so Vast a consideration: reduc'd into its naturall bignesse as to Us consists but of 6 or 8 Persons and if wee are rich, a few Acres of Ground more than our neighbour possesses...[1].

He continues that "life is a 'probation,'" speaks of one being "entangled with the birdlime of the world," and refers to Anne Conway's life as a "perpetuall

[1] Brit. Mus. *Addit. MSS.* 23215, f. 50.

crosse and self denyall." He closes with the words that nothing would make him more happy than to see her.

Whilst in Rome Baines met "Mr Boyle" (Roger Broghill, eldest son of the first Earl of Orrery) and his tutor Mr Hall. Baines writes[1] of the illness of the Pope, and of the trouble into which a Dutch Baron got himself. The latter killed one of the Pope's guards in trying to force his way into the ceremony of washing the Pilgrims' feet on Holy Thursday,

this year performed by Cardinall Barbarino as the Pope is sick with ulcer of the bladder and very likely to die; all the prisoners are removed out of the common gaoles into the strong castell of Saint Angelo for feare as soon as the Pope is dead the keepers let open the prison dores, otherwise the people would break them open.

At this time, too, Baines sent some presents to the Conways, and Finch evidently opened Baines' letter to Conway and supplemented his friend's description of the articles, for he writes:

The Doctor sent your Lordship these from Rome and he forgott to mention in his letter; Brescia Pistole Barrells, he sent your Lordship, with the cap (one of the Great Duke's). Those things he sends my sister which were given him by the Great Duke are of singular use for her that keeps her bed being very ingenious contrivances to sit at all heights in the bed and have the use of a table. It goes upon screws, and everything is to be unscrewed; the glasse within the bed pan is to be taken out by unscrewing the handle and taking the handle quite off (*sic*) for then it opens. All the other screws are obvious enough[2].

Anne Conway was at this time still in very poor health and Finch was quite correct in his opinion, expressed to Lord Conway, that nothing could be done for her:

...I resolved not to write till I could send the studyed Advice of Dr Baines for my sister: for though he be my Dear friend your Lordship must not thinke it my partiality, but my persuasion that when I tell your Lordship that He nor no man can cure her. My Lord I send it here to your Lordship enclos'd: and I hope God Almighty has strengthen'd him to be usefull where above all things in this World I dare swear he wishes to doe good[3].

Henry More induced Anne Conway to try many doctors, but some of these must be placed in the class of quacks. Valentine Greatrakes, "the renowned Irish stroker," treated her, and Viscount Conway writes to his secretary Rawdon in high hope that this man would cure his wife of her headaches (Rawdon papers). But in spite of all attempted remedies Anne Conway suffered terribly, and only death itself brought a happy release.

In the same letter Finch gives the outline of a dispute, which had arisen through the fact that a Captain Hubbard had arrived at the port of Livorno with a squadron and had not saluted the port. This was the occasion for addresses to the Grand Duke, as a protest was made against the English Captain's sin of omission. Finch's plea was that the guns ashore never returned

---

[1] Brit. Mus. *Addit. MSS.* 23215, f. 52. [2] *Ibid.* f. 46 b.
[3] *Ibid.* f. 54, Florence, July 2-12, 1667.

Plate VI

From portrait by Carlo Dolci at Burley-on-the-Hill

a salute, if given, and finally the matter was settled by the forts giving back the salute, gun for gun, "nine apiece." The Ambassador Finch considered this a tremendous concession on the part of Tuscany and describes the return of the salute as "a respect beyond all the Kings of Christendom." A cypher letter to Conway goes into more detail about this incident.

From hints in the letters and from facts that have been mentioned already, we learn that the health of the friends was not always of the best. Heneage Finch mentions this matter in writing to his son: "...I am glad your uncle did so soon recover his indisposition...I would to God Dr Baynes were freed from the payns of the stone, and from all apprehensions of its retourne[1]." How often has not the "racking" stone gone with, and been part of, the life of a hard student! Baines himself describes this attack of stone in a letter to Conway dated "Flor. Aug. 11, 1667":

...my tardancy in answering it proceeded not from the want of duty or sence I had of so high an obligation: but from the immensity of the distemper of the stone I then laboured under: voyding in the space of eighteen dayes at least eight or nine hundred stones from my right kidney, which leaving mee very weake...but now beyond all men's expectation and my owne reason I am thanks bee to God in appearance returned to my former condition. God knows how long it will last[2].

I can find no trace of any pictures of Finch and Baines except those now hanging at Burley-on-the-Hill. Besides the portrait of *Sir John Finch at his Studies* by Van Hoogstraaten there are two more of him at Burley and also two of his friend Baines. Sir John never lived at Burley, for the present magnificent house was built by Daniel Finch about 1700, some time after Sir John's death. The portraits were inherited by Daniel, and these and a large number of the books of Finch and Baines were taken to Burley. Miss Pearl Finch, in her book *History of Burley-on-the-Hill*, mentions only three portraits, which have as their subject either Finch or Baines, but two more have been brought to light since her catalogue of the pictures was compiled. All the pictures were cleaned after the fire and no doubt the names on these two have come out. They are of "the Doctors" as much younger men (Plates IV and V) "and are evidently the work of some competent English painter of the period[3]."

Present members of the Finch family tell me that there has been a tradition since 1750 that the two splendid portraits (Plates VI and VII) are by Carlo Dolci (1616–1686). He was a Florentine painter, was an extremely religious man, and for the most part painted pictures of Christ or of members of the Holy Family. However he painted more than one portrait of himself, one of the Archbishop of Florence, and several others. These portraits of Finch and Baines are unsigned, nor do either of them mention these pictures in their letters.

[1] *Finch Report* (Hist. MSS. Comm.), vol. 1, p. 467.
[2] Brit. Mus. *Addit. MSS.* 23215, f. 58.
[3] Lionel Cust and Archibald Ma'loch, *loc. cit.*

By the merest chance I found a reference in one of Gio. Targioni Tozzetti's works (*Atti e Memorie inedite dell' Accademia del Cimento e Notizie Aneddote dei Progressi delle Scienze in Toscana*, Firenze, MDCCLXXX) to a sketch of the life of Carlo Dolci[1] by Filippo Baldinucci (1624-1696) which proves that this artist painted portraits of Finch and Baines. There seems little reason to doubt that the portraits at Burley to which the family tradition is attached are the ones spoken of by Baldinucci. I quote the passage at length, as other pictures by Carlo Dolci and bought by Finch are referred to.

...Equally with every other work of his at Florence was esteemed the *Erodiade* [Herodias] with the head of John Baptist, a more than half life size figure executed for the Marquis Ronuccini, with the other picture of *David* holding the dead head of the Philistine Giant as a pendant. Nevertheless of the *Erodiades* he painted a second and then a third: the second was for John Finch, Minister in Florence of H.M. the King of England, to whom the said Minister presented it. For the same Finch, Dolci also painted, as pendants the *David with Goliath's Head*, and a *Saint Mary Magdalene* which were presented to the Queen In addition he painted Sir John Finch's portrait and that of his most confidential attaché Doctor Fava which were so successful that they may be said without exaggeration to be his master-pieces. When seen in England they made such a sensation that many noblemen and gentlemen of that nation, on their way through Florence had their portraits painted by him. Of these gentlemen the name of one has been preserved viz. John Broghim.

For the two portraits painted for the English Minister, Carlino in addition to the hundred ducats stipulated, received a gift of twenty-five Spanish doubloons.

Finch had only one "most confidential attaché," and "Fava" must be regarded as a misreading of a MS. for "Baines." Tozzetti in his book on the *Accademia del Cimento* writes of "Tommaso Forbes" instead of "Tommaso Baines." "Fava" is Italian for "bean," but it seems very unlikely that an attempt was made to translate "Baines" into Italian! The name "Broghim" seems to be a mistake, but it is doubtful if we could replace it by "Broghill" (*i.e.* of the Boyle family).

The *Herodias with St John's Head* and the *S. Mary Magdalene* are amongst a list of the paintings in the possession of King James II, and they were amongst the pictures lent to exhibitions by both George IV and William IV. They are now at Windsor Castle. I have been unable to trace the *David with Goliath's Head*, and Lionel Cust, Esquire, C.V.O., Surveyor of the King's Pictures and Works of Art, knows nothing of this painting, but suggests that Queen Catharine of Braganza may have retained it as her private property.

A mezzotint was engraved by J. Faber from the painting of *Herodias* in 1728 and there is one also at the British Museum of an almost identical painting by Carlo Dolci in Dresden. Two of the three pictures of *Herodias*, mentioned in the passage quoted above, may thus be traced.

Mr Cust[2] writes of the portraits of Finch and Baines, "they are excellent

---

[1] *Notizie de' Professori del disegno*...Tom. VI, p. 503. This work of Baldinucci was published, in the year 1717, after his death.   [2] *Loc. cit.*

Plate VII

From portrait by Carlo Dolci at Burley-on-the-Hill

in every way, treated with a breadth and sobriety of colour which one would connect with the Dutch school of the period rather than with the Italian."

In the portrait of Sir John he is holding an Italian document dated from "Firenze" and addressed to the Grand Duke. The intention of representing Finch as the English Ambassador is evident.

Carlo Dolci, we must conclude for other reasons, was known to Finch, for in one of his commonplace books Finch has written some notes "On colours" and in these he quotes Carlo Dolci's opinions several times. There is a signed picture by Carlo Dolci at Burley representing the head of the Infant Christ; this no doubt was bought by Finch, for on his return alone from Turkey he procured many paintings in Italy and Florence and "four of Carlo Dolci." *Christ breaking Bread* by Carlo Dolci hangs in Burleigh House "by Stamford town," the seat of the Marquis of Exeter.

In the other portrait Baines is seated at a table on which are several books. He is immediately engaged on Plato and Aristotle and there are other slips of paper in books marked "Euclid" and "Hippocr...." Baines is apparently extracting passages from Plato and Aristotle. One of his note-books preserved at Burley is entirely devoted to this work. His method of note-taking is worth recording and might well be followed by the student to-day, had he the leisure time of Baines.

Short Collections

Out of Plato and Aristotle: of Plato there is his booke entitled politicus; his ten books de Republica, and his Thirteen bookes de legibus, the last of which Hee calls ἐπινομίς; out of Aristotle there is his eight bookes de Republica, his two bookes de Cura Rei Familiaris, his ten bookes de Moribus, his two bookes entitled Eudemia, his booke de virtutibus et vitiis and his Rhetoricke.

In taking of these notes I have observed that method which I have donne heretofore in others, and shall allwayes doe hereafter.

1. In reading an ancient author as Plato and Aristotle, I take notice of Knowne important truths, though common, chiefly out of gratitude that I may in private thoughts, and publicke Discourse pay my respects to the first origen and there is in it the pompe and glory of learning.

2. I take notice of truths which though I knew either in part or in whole before, yet they are more plumply, scientifically and handsomely conveyed, and in this there is both profitt and pleasure.

3. I take notice of truths which I never knew before and perhaps in these I am allwayes larger then the Author where the case points for my owne instruction, and carry a constant eie (*sic*) whether in his following bookes hee speakes any further to that point. And in these there is abundance of profitt and abundance of pleasure, for in a fruitfull braine how much does once (*sic*) certaine truth branch.

4. Lastly I take notice of egregious errors: partly that I may shew them others to decline, but chiefly that in farther reading of Him I may easelyer (*sic*) perceive the lesser declinations from those more palpable, by which I decline the straining of my braine to give a candid interpretation of that which was meaned amisse, which otherwise in charity I ought to doe to every famous man: καὶ ταῦτα μὲν ταῦτα: atque haec de his.

Finch had scarcely begun his term as Resident at Florence when his friends sought out positions for him in England. As early as June, 1665, Conway[1] writes a very interesting letter to him and states that he and Heneage Finch were angry with Lord Arlington, as the latter had failed to fulfil his promise towards Sir John.

...he promised this should be redeemed, and would have done it very opportunely upon the death of Mr O'Neale, of the King's bedchamber, had not your being knighted rendered you incapable thereof, but his lordship has made amends by the employment you now enjoy: his lordship is a power of the greatest honour and merit that ever was, and you will find yourself more happy under his protection than if you had choice of the Court, for his power and reediness to oblige is greater than any man's...I hope ultimately to bring you in to succeed Sec. Morice in his office which will be more eligible than removing to Constantinople....

Another letter in 1668 shows that it was intended that Finch should enter Parliament upon his return[2]. Viscount Conway wrote to his brother-in-law Sir John Finch in February, 1668:

...Lord Arlington intends to have you chosen a Parliament man before you arrive; by that method you will come into court advantageously. I advise your return by France, because you will be first employed in foreign affairs. You will have the advantage of coming into a court where there is not one man of ability.

In 1667 Heneage Finch was still "an unsuccessful suitor" for Finch's return.

In March, 1666–7[3], Finch wrote to Lord Conway about his wishes for the future and about his dissatisfaction with his life in Italy at that time. These letters are partly in cypher, but fortunately the keys were found amongst the manuscripts at the British Museum and almost all the words can be deciphered by their aid.

...But my Lord as I am eternally obliged to your Lordship's kindnesse, which endeavours to begett me an Interest in Lord Ashley [? Arlington] yet I must needs say I find so little application to buisnesse at court and particularly in Lord Ashley [?] that I know not how to hope an esteeme from Lord Ashley unlesse his Lordship could find something to employ mee in, that might ease his [?] owne trouble. And indeed my Lord though I have the strongest desires imaginable to retourne home being desirous if possible to enjoy your Lordship's and my sisters company, I having little satisfaction to spend my time in a charge whose dignity cannot be supported with the allowance of Sir John Finch. Yet my Lord to use the freedome your Lordship's affection permits; I had rather at my retourne retire from the noyse of the world and enjoy my owne thoughts free from subjection, then have office at court void of application and buisnesse. Yet I had rather undertake anything then to be banished any longer from seeing your Lordship and my sister. Nay though to be sent to Constantinople were a charge of great gaine yet I would not buy that charge with the affliction so long a separation would create mee. But anything is better then my present condition in which I neither enjoy myselfe nor anything else.

In a later cypher letter Finch writes:

I doe perfectly abhorr the thoughts of goeing to Constantinople in so much that upon the unfortunate marriage of My Lord Maydston [Winchilsea's son] and the Disappointment

---

[1] *Calendar of State Papers—Domestic, Addenda,* 1660–1670, p. 701. June? 1665.
[2] *Ibid.* 1667–1668, p. 258.   [3] *Addit. MSS.* 23215.

that my Lord of Winchilsea must have of providing for his younger children I persuaded him to stay at least seven years longer.

In the same letter Finch gives an account of another incident in his political life in Italy, which is found in the Rawlinson MSS. (see note on page 45).

In my last I gave your Lordship an Account with how much difficulty I struggl'd with the Pope here, who would by his Nuncio have suppress'd the Protestant Preaching, and was so exorbitant as to pretend to silence my chaplayn in my own house, which ridiculous extravagancy though I soon quashed, yet I find that the factory in my absence will hardly be allowed that freedome: I therefore acquainted my Lord Arlington with it; and told his Lordship that I knew no expedient but my residing as many Moneths at Livorno as I had wont to do at Florence. And I told his Lordship that I held it not reasonable that His Majesty onely for the sake of the factory should be at the Expense, which would be great in my taking another house here which would be at least £120 per Annum, another in the country which every Merchant to avoid this bad Ayr has; and the necessity of multiply'd Entertainments where so vast a number of English were whom I must not be oblig'd by: if I mean to govern. My Lord if his Lordship pitches upon this expedient of my residing at Livorno though in matter of Religion...[*three letters illegible through a hole in the paper*] Lord Ashley [? Arlington] is not so much concerned as Viscount Conway[1] who writes very warmly about it. I beseech your Lordship to insinuate to Lord Ashley [?], that I cannot under double the Expense stay as long in Livorno, as hitherto I have done at Florence. But I fearing the Warr is likely to last longer then Viscount Conway wishes, Lord Ashley [?] having told mee that the Treaty at the Hague was propounded without assurance of being accepted and I fear with a certainty if being rejected to the great disreputation of Sir John Finch[1] abroad, I would not have new resolutions to prejudice mee either as to my stay or to my allowance if I am putt upon new occasions of expence.

In 1670 the Grand Duke of Tuscany died and a letter describes Finch's visit to condole with the Dowager Duchess forty days after her husband's decease, and to congratulate her on her son's succession to the title[2].

[1] In an ordinary letter these words would read "you" and "me," but the numbers "13" and "10" are cypher for "Viscount Conway" and "Sir John Finch."
[2] *Calendar of State Papers—Domestic*, 1670, p. 332. July 14th.

CHAPTER VII

ENGLAND AGAIN

In August, 1670, Sir John's letter of revocation to England was despatched by Lord Arlington, who hoped "to get Sir John Finch into the House[1]." Apparently Finch and Baines did not arrive in England till July, 1671[2].

Baines was again in poor health and More writes to Lady Conway, "C.C.C.," 11th May, 1672:

...Mrs Foxcroft writt me so melancholy a letter that I thought Dr Baines was about ready to give up the ghost, so that I was surprised when I heard he was come to Cambridge. Though his leggs fayl him yett his tongue walks as free as ever, and is very good company on that account and really I phancy his mind is of a better frame then heretofore and Sr John really is the best company in the world. But it is a good thing to be pleased with any of these things, because the enjoyment of them is not in our power, but it is like a flash of evening lightning as they are all dispersed to their occasions and leave me alone....

There is no reference in the *Calendar of State Papers* to the effect that Finch entered Parliament, but throughout this stay in England he acted on the Council for Plantations[3]. "Warrant for renewal of the Commission of the Council for Plantations, inviting Sir William Hickman in place of Sir John Finch appointed ambassador to the Ottoman Empire, on the death of Sir Dan. Harvey." In the volume *Cal. of State Papers—Colonial*, 1669–1674, an account is given of the formation and purposes of this Commission, and, under later dates, an account of their work.

Finch and Baines resided at the Inner Temple with Heneage Finch. In the autumn of 1672 Finch was recommended by the King to be Ambassador at the Ottoman Court in place of Sir Daniel Harvey deceased, who had succeeded Winchilsea at Constantinople.

It seemed very possible at this time that "the Doctors" would now be separated for a long period, if not for the remainder of their days, and that whilst Finch, on his way to Turkey, would settle some dispute at Leghorn[4], Baines would be starting for the New World, for an interesting note from Sir John Finch to Williamson tells us, "Lord Arlington desires you to remind him to constitute Dr Thomas Baines of the Commissioners the King is resolved to send

---

[1] *Calendar of State Papers—Domestic*, 1670, p. 389. Aug. 23rd, 1670.   [2] *Ibid.* 1671, July 18th.
[3] *Ibid.* 1672-1673, p. 114. Nov. 2nd, 1672.   [4] *Ibid.* 1673, p. 107, March(?).

to New England[1]." Possibly Baines was to be one of the Commissioners whom the King was to appoint.

Recommended that the King send Commissioners to New England to examine the differences concerning the boundaries of the Massachusetts and the rest of the colonies, that the Commissioners be despatched to arrive before the end of next October, as ships cannot without danger come into harbour there after that time[2].

Ferdinand Gorges, Esq., had previously petitioned the King, claiming the province of Maine inherited from his father, but which the Governor of Massachusetts had laid hold of whilst he (Gorges) "was away in King's father's service in the late wars." However this proposed appointment was not confirmed, and Sir John and Sir Thomas did not part company but set out on their travels together once more.

Baines was knighted on 24th May, 1672, at Whitehall[3] before he went to Constantinople, and not on his setting out for Florence, as is generally stated.

It was at first intended that Finch and Baines should leave England soon after the former's appointment and he tells of it in a letter to Conway written about 10th November, 1672.

The last weeke I acquainted your Lordship that His Majesty having made me His Ambassador to the Gran Signor I had kissed his hand upon it, on Thursday the 9th Instant I delivered the King's letter to the Turky Company and they immediately and cheerfully acknowledged me under that Character. So that now within twelve dayes I suppose I shall beginn my Voyage. The Duke has bin pleased to promise me a ship to Constantinople, and a strong Convoy to the Merchants: of which there is need, advice being come that the "Dutch are putt to sea with 22 Men of War, 50 to 70 Guns, and double Mann'd and 10 fire ships." Sir Thomas Osburn is a gentleman I have so true an Honour for: that I will Endeavour his Service to the utmost of my Capacity, and I will assure you Sr Thomas Baines and I have so discoursed this matter with Mr Attorney [Heneage Finch] that He who has a reverence for Sir Thomas Osborne more then for any Gentleman in England, has promised us to own that concern and Push it on to the uttermost and I intend before I goe, to gett them to Discourse the matter and I hope all our wishes may succeed; But of all things I will be least responsible for marriages.

Sir Thomas Osburn was at this time Lord Treasurer, and it seems probable that the "marriage" in question was that of Daniel, Finch's nephew, for he married Lady Essex Rich on 16th June, 1674. However Finch and Baines were delayed in their departure until the beginning of the summer. Baines wrote a long and interesting letter to Anne Conway from the Inner Temple, 19th December, 1672[4], thanking her for the hospitality at Ragley where he and Finch had spent "seven monneths." After stating that he had been in bed for three weeks with the gout, he describes the intended missions to Leghorn and to Geneva ("with an angry message from his Majesty"), and he goes on to speak of the appointment to Turkey and the manner of life they hope to lead there.

---

[1] *Cal. of State Papers—Domestic*, 1673 p. 107.
[2] *Cal. of State Papers—Colonial*, 1671, March 5th.
[3] Shaw's *Book of Knights*.
[4] Brit. Mus. *Addit. MSS.* 23215, f. 69.

Finch guaranteed to stay with the Turkey Company for six years at a salary of "ten thousand mighty dollars," equivalent, Baines says, to £2800 a year. In a later letter Baines speaks of Finch's liberality. "This is the salary of the man that usually what Hee gets with his right hand, Hee scatters with his left[1]." The Turkey Company was to pay his Chaplain £100, and would meet the expenses of coaches and retinue, should Finch have to make journeys.

Baines describes the arrangements Finch was making for their sojourn in Turkey:

...His family I adjudge will be about thirtye, two pages and twelve footmen in livery, which he hath made very rich. One livery serving Him the whole six years because they weare them only when they goe out, and when they come back they putt them off. As for his Wine the Turk allows Him seven thousand measures of wine custome free He in his own house can spend but two thousand so that selling the other it will pay the whole cost of His wine. Other Provisions as I am informed eccessive cheap save only butter deer, Partridges being worth about a penny apiece a Pheasant or a Capon about five pence or six pence: Mutton veal and Beef, five farthings or three half pence the Bushell and fish of all Sorts extraordinary good and extraordinarye Cheap, a Gentleman assuring me that a fresh Sturgeon of an Ell long he did see it sould for a crown. And it is well that all things are thus for your Brother layes out here in England in order to His Embassye and other things no lesse then two thousand five Hundred Pound, His cloaths are very rich, His plate amounts to thirteen hundred Pound, more by half then ever any Ambassador carry'd, which He doth that at an Entertainment He might not blush, knowing very well that when He is invited by the Emperor, French, or Venetian Ambassador they will be all serv'd in Plate, and He is resolved not to be inferiour to any of them, and indeed in publick things where the Honour of the Nation is concern'd, Parcimony is a great fault.

Now as to our pleasure during our stay there, we have contriv'd it thus. Our conversation shall be, with the craftyest and most ingenuous (*sic*) Jesuit we can find, with the sobriest and most stayd Patriarchiall man of the Greek Church to whom if your Ladyship please to add the arrantest and cunningest Knave amonge the Jewes we can light upon, say our conversation is made Compleat; a house we shall take upon the black sea, and keep a barge a purpose to carry us thither and to go a fishing in as often as we shall take delight...and because Turkey is no place for Coaches we supply that defect with a couple of very handsome Saddans which we shall carry over with us....Thus we continue to sweeten our stay there as many ways as we can suggest, not leaving behind us our Library to entertain us in our most sober thoughts....but that that contributes no little matter to the pleasure and content of this Voyage is the security of our pay: being no court pay, needs no sollicitation of friends, but falls out as certain as if I had a hundred Pound Rent chardg'd a year out of the Mannor of Ragley: so that there is nothing of bitternesse in it seeing that our friends Company....

In another letter[2], to Lord Conway, Baines writes that the goods and servants are already shipped upon "one of his Majesty's frigates the *Centurion* a ship of fifty-two guns, having obtained also a catch to waite upon Her, which upon occasion turns into a fire shipp a great security and convenience against the Hazards of the sea, and those of an enemy which ought to be provided against." One Charles Wylde was the commander of this ship and his journal

---

[1] Brit. Mus. *Addit. MSS.* 23215, f. 71, 16th April, 1673.   [2] *Ibid.* f. 71, April, 1673.

of the voyage to Constantinople is in the British Museum[1]. It gives the position of the ship day by day, records escapes from privateers, describes the hearty way in which Finch was received at the various landings, and contains several water-colour studies of the coast lines they passed and water-colour maps of some of the ports.

Finch had not found his sister at all well whilst he was in England, and though she was under the care of Van Helmont, for whom years before Finch had not a good word to say, he makes no complaint on this occasion. A letter from the Inner Temple in August, 1672, to Conway reveals his deep feeling at the thought of Anne's poor health:

...I met this morning at my Lord Arlington's Van Helmont and having made with all imaginable modesty the most important demands I could thinke of relating to my Dear sister's health: I was struck with such a dampe upon his answers that I had scarce courage enough to disguise my sorrow, to negotiaite with my Lord Arlington, who I fear discovered in me a perturbation his Lordship could not guesse at the cause of. But since I am free from those Eyes that gave me Subjection, I hope my own have given part of that constant Tribute they must ever pay to my Dear Sister's affliction or the memory of it or her. I am I protest more reduc'd to an indifferency of life finding the greatest comfort I ever promised myselfe in it (the happinesse of her Conversation) snatch'd from me, if I protest this World has little left either of hopes or fears for me. I dare not write to her whom Van Helmont himselfe represents incapable of reading what I write, My Lord I will send my Soul to her but not words, that weake interpretation of it, for I very well knowe that no words can convey my sense, and if they did, they will only embitter our mutuall sufferings....

When Finch set out for Turkey, he must have realized that there was small chance of his seeing his sister alive again.

Finch writes from the Inner Temple, 14th May, 1673, to Lord Conway[2] that he was to "take yacht at Dover Tuesday the 24th," and writes again on the 14th to say farewell, should he never return.

I am now leaving England...This is the third time I have left my Native Soyl: If God Almighty make me so happy as to return once more to your Lordship, I shall then thinke it is time to fix at home and leave of (*sic*) all thoughts of further wandering. But [if] my life by its period abroad putts one to my Travell I beseech your Lordship to believe that you have lost the most faythfull and zealous servant the World yet was ever possessed of....

He travelled into Italy across France and visited Montreuil, Paris, Turin, Genoa, Florence, and met the ship *Centurion* at Leghorn.

Whilst in Paris he investigated a new method of stopping bleeding and described it in a letter to his nephew Daniel[3]:

'Tis now six weeks since in Paris they have found out a secret of stopping any bleeding (nay though an artery be cutt in sunder) by laying upon it a linen cloth dipped in a certain water. The King of France gave the inventor 2,000 crowns; and now the King and all the great officers in the army are never without a viall of this water. There are five persons at present who have become masters of the secret: the experiment I would need see made before me in

---

[1] Brit. Mus. *Sloane MSS.* 2439.   [2] Brit. Mus. *Addit. MSS.* 23215, f. 73.
[3] *Finch Report* (Hist. MSS. Comm.), vol. II, p. 11. 17–27th June, 1673.

my lodgings, and a doctor and two chirurgeons came with a dog, but Carpenter [F.'s secretary] not cutting the crural artery, the blood was soon stopped by the water. But Sir Thomas, another dog being sent for, cutt the artery himselfe and the dog dyed by the effusion of bloud, but not so but that the water shewed a very strange effect; for it preserved the dog in life for severall hours, and of all things I have yet seen to stop bloud is the most efficacious. The water is insipid, for I tasted it suspecting it to be caustick, but I am apt to believe as Sir Thomas conjectured, that it is a destillation of opium or poppy with the *aqua exspermare ranarum*. 'Tis of great use in gunshotts where remedi's of stopping bloud cannot be readily had; I bought as many glasses of it as cost two louis d'or....

They sailed from Leghorn for Malta 29th November, 1673, and arrived there on the 14th of December, as Finch's note-book and Captain Wylde's journal record. Finch made some remarks to the King on religion, and made notes on the "Religion" (*i.e.* Order of St John), revenues, fortifications, etc. They landed at Smyrna in January, 1673-4, and finally reached Adrianople towards the end of March.

CHAPTER VIII

CONSTANTINOPLE

Again Baines was allowed to enjoy "the salary and other emoluments" of his office as Professor at Gresham College[1] when he accompanied Finch to Turkey. Some years before, Winchilsea had desired that Baines should go out to him as his physician at Constantinople. But on this occasion neither Finch nor Baines ever states what position Baines was to occupy in Turkey and there is nothing to indicate that it was in any way an official one.

In the Rawlinson Collection[2] at the Bodleian Library there is a manuscript containing instructions to Finch on his appointment to Turkey and another such in the British Museum[3].

Mahomet IV was then Sultan of Turkey, and during his reign he accomplished much for the Ottoman Empire; he concluded the war with Venice, which had lasted for twenty-seven years, by subjecting the island of Candia; the town of Kamenitz, the key of Poland, was in his hands; he reduced the Cossacks to obedience, and he imposed a new tribute on all Poland.

In Knolles' *Turkish History*[4] is given an account of Finch's arrival in Turkey:

> About the 18th of March Sir John Finch Arriv'd at Constantinople, & some few days after in the absence of the Grand Seignior & Visier, had Audience of the Chimacam, to whom he said:
> "I am come Ambassador from Charles the 2nd King of England, Scotland, France, and Ireland, sole Lord and Sovereign of all the Seas, Territories and Possessions in the East & West Indies, Defender of the Christian Faith against all that worship Idols or Images: To the most powerful & Mighty Emperor of the East, to maintain that Peace, which hath been so useful, and that Commerce which hath been so profitable to this Empire: For the continuance whereof I promis you in my Station, to contribute what I can, and I promis myself that you will do the Like in yours."

Finch's interest in the work of the Royal Society has already been noticed, and amongst the papers that were at Burley, is one communication from Oldenburgh, the Secretary of the Society at that time, to Sir John Finch[5]:

---

[1] *Calendar of State Papers—Domestic*, 1673, p. 238. 12th May.
[2] *Rawl. MSS.* A. 256, p. 51, and letters of revocation, Nov. 1680, pp. 253 and 261.
[3] *Addit. MSS.* 2893, p. 167.
[4] Ed. 1701, vol. II, p. 206. Paul Rycaut, who had been the Earl of Winchilsea's secretary at Constantinople, made considerable additions to this history.
[5] *Finch Report* (Hist. MSS. Comm.), vol. II, p. 6.

1. To take notice of the directions and enquiries relating both to land and sea, published in the *Phil. Trans.* Nos. XI and XXIV, of each of which a copy accompanies these.

2. To excite the English Consuls, Vice Consuls and factors in Turkey the Levant and Egypt, to impart all the observable of nature and art, that have occurred or shall occur to their observation.

Then follow various questions about the Red Sea and where the Israelites might have passed over, about the quicksands and how far from their point of passage is the place where are bitter waters. About *Rusma* [a powder to remove hairs], where in Turkey and in what quantities it is found; about opium and whether the Turks take it "for strength and courage" and also give it to their horses and dromedaries when they are faint with travelling and what is the greatest dose any man or woman is known to have taken; about mummies; about the frequency of earthquakes in Zant and Zephalonia; how to procure a good description of the hills of Turkey; about people living to the age of 120 in Arabia; whether the fruits, herbs, etc. of Cyprus are naturally saltish; what is the art of tempering steel in Damascus; about the Aqueducts of Solyman and about the breeding of Angora goats. How far Finch was able to answer any of these questions we do not know, but certainly he published no papers in the *Phil. Trans. of the Roy. Soc.* The enquiries, however, serve to show what "stretched the pia mater" of that group of men who composed the Royal Society so soon after its foundation.

There are practically no letters amongst the Burley papers relating to the early years of the friends' stay in Turkey, but from the length of the epistles to the Conways[1] they must have spent many hours in the study of the country and of its religion. There is a very lengthy communication to "My most D.D.," as Finch called his sister, on the customs and religion, and the latter subject is discussed in a letter to Lord Conway, 4–14th February, 1674–5, under the headings (1) One God, (2) No Wine, (3) Liberty of Conscience, (4) Four Wives, and Finch adds that "by these four principles Mahommedanism has overspread so great a part of the world."

Before 1677 perhaps Finch's most important political work in Turkey was accomplished. Fortunately the much-travelled Covel (1638–1722) (afterwards Master of Christ's) was in Turkey. He had been there as Chaplain to Sir Daniel Harvey and remained on with Finch and Baines until 1679, as Chaplain to the Levant Company, and he describes[2] the trip, which he, and "the Ambassador and Chevalier" (*i.e.* Finch and Baines), made to Adrianople in the interest of the Capitulations of 1676 which Finch secured for the Company. These capitulations did much for the security of trading and property in the Levant. One

[1] *Loc. cit.*
[2] *Early Voyages and Travels in the Levant*, II. Extracts from the diaries of Dr John Covel, 1670–1679, printed for the Hakluyt Society, pp. 190 and 191.

clause granted liberty to export from Smyrna and elsewhere two ships' lading of fruit annually for the King's own use in his kitchen[1].

They travelled in true Oriental magnificence. Covel says "My Lord's [Finch's] horses furniture were set out with jewels and pearls most gloriously," but the contrast of this with conditions at Adrianople could hardly be more striking and Covel does not mince words in describing them: "The house we first were all allotted was the damn'dest confounded place that ever mortal man was put into: it was a Jewes house, not half big enough to hold my Lord's family, a mere nest of fleas and cimici [*i.e.* bugs] and rats and mice and stench surrounded with whole kennells of nasty, beastly Jewes." The plague was rife at this time, and Finch and his party had to betake themselves to tents[2], and several persons died.

Covel was a great friend of both Finch and Baines, and in 1676-7[3] Finch gave him a bill of exchange for one hundred dollars drawn upon Livorno as a present with which he was to buy books. Covel returned to England in 1679 and Baines writes a very affectionate letter to him[4]:

...I was never good at shooting flying, and from that youth to this day was never good at a movable mutable subject: but I allways look'd about me to see where I could fix my point, which found out, I moved upon that and then rung as many Changes as I could. In like manner my delight is to see the subject fix'd to whome I talk or write, as well as that upon which I speake.

Then Sir you being arrived in your native Country, Give me leave to give you the Welcome, or *Buon Pro* of the enjoyments you have had in the Lap of our Common old Mother Cambridge, where you are dally'd and Caressed by her...God have him [More] & you & all of us in His Holy Protection and Preserve us that wee may once meet at a Philosophical Banquett, I rest, Dear Sir, etc.

The correspondence of Finch with Anne Conway was most remarkable; and Lamb's affection for his sister was not a deeper one. There is scarcely a break in the chain of letters from Finch to Anne Viscountess Conway except when she was so ill that Sir John wrote only to her husband with the hope that he would give her the news. Her letters to him are few and far between amongst the Conway papers at the British Museum, but nowhere could one find more protestations of affection than in Finch's epistles and apparently he kept no secret from her. Donne's line

Sir, more than kisses, letters mingle soules;

seems so true in the case of John and Anne.

In November, 1678, a letter from More brought the news that Anne had become a Quaker. This event receives much attention in Ward's *Life of Henry More*, and the author tries to seek an explanation of this conversion to another

---

[1] Vide *Calendar of State Papers—Domestic*, 1676, Sept. 1, p. 308.
[2] North's *Life of Dudley North*, "Epistle from Adrianople."
[3] Brit. Mus. *Addit. MSS.* 22910, f. 122. [4] *Ibid.* f. 192.

faith than that of More, who it will be remembered was so great a friend of his "Heroine Pupil" and is said to have dedicated one of his treatises to her, but in the bibliography I can only find that he dedicated one to Lord Conway. He spent so much of his time at Ragley. She was now in bed in the last year of her years-long illness and Finch does not upbraid her, but he could not refrain from a discussion on the singular pronoun as a form of address[1].

But since you seem to effect the Words Thou and Thee: I can easily reassume that Dialect, But at the same time I must tell Thee my Dear, That all words being themselves equally Innocent they being guilty of no Crime but when they are made Conveyors of what is in Truth contrary to the message they carry: To confine ourselves to any sort of Words is the restraining of Human Nature to What it is not oblig'd. Thou and Thee being as capable of conveying untruths as Right Honourable or My Lady, or Madam. Most certain it is that God having made man the superior part of Creation, by giving Him a Power of Discoursing by Language, Which rendered man alone capable of Divine precepts, all which are convey'd by Words....

This philosophy of words is then continued over a large page and Finch cannot understand that "the Friends" laid such a stress on the form of address.

...I must really professe unto Thee that I cannot but wonder and that very much, how it comes to passe that that sort of People which in England are commonly call'd Quakers, and originally thought to have many well meaning, though mistaken Persons amongst them, should, owning it as a Principle that they are against all Forms, bring themselves to a Form....

Finch closes his letter with a benediction. In the British Museum[2] there are several letters to Anne Conway from a group of Quakers, William Penn, Charles Lloyd, Thos. Bromley, Joseph Cooper, George Keith, Giles Skene.

Tozzetti quotes from a draft of a letter written by Prince Leopold of Tuscany to Sir John Finch. They wrote extremely complimentary letters in those days, but the feelings expressed in the letter are apparently quite genuine and Finch was greatly missed by the scientific spirits of Tuscany. Tozzetti[3] gives the date as 1668, but in that year Finch was at Florence as Ambassador and there is no reason to believe that he left that city. Why should the Prince write as if Finch were at a great distance and out of touch with the scientific circle? The Grand Duke Ferdinand II was evidently still alive and it is still more difficult to date the letter.

Al Sig. Cav. Gio. Finchio, 21 Marzo 1668 ab Incarnatione. Il gusto con che ricevo la Lettera di V.S. del 21 del corrente, è proporzionato alla stima che fo del suo merito, e l'espressioni ch' Ella mi fa del suo affetto, sono accolte volentieri dai sentimenti non dissimili, che verso di Lei conservo nell' animo. Al Serenissimo Granduca ho rappresentato quanto V.S. mi scrive, in attestazione della memoria amorevolissima che Ella ne conserva, e credami che S.A. ne ha grandemente goduto, tenendo anche da lontano nel dovuto pregio la singolare virtù di V.S. e mi ha imposto di farlene indubitata fede. Con non differenti dettami, applaudono al suo valore il Serenissimo Principe (Cosimo III) ed il Sig. Principe Mattias, a' quali non ho parimente lasciato di partecipare l'istessa Lettera di V.S., e rendasi

---

[1] Brit. Mus. *Addit. MSS.* 23215, f. 94. [2] *Ibid.* 23217.
[3] *Atti e Memorie dell' Accademia del Cimento*...Firenze, MDCCLXXX, Tom. 1, p. 274.

pure certa, che appresso a tutti di questa Casa. Ell' è in così degno concetto, che non è mai per cancellarlo intervallo di tempo, o di luogo. Io poi mi contento d' esser compreso tra gli altri, per non mostrar pretensione di distinguermi; ma Ella può ben' assicurarsi, che nell' amarla e stimarla non cedo a nessuno. Non mi giugne nuovo che V.S. sia costà applicata in operazioni virtuose, perchè io so che queste sono inseparabili dal suo gran talento; e mi giova sperare, ch' Ella non lascerà di parteciparle a chi ne vive con desiderio. Veramente in quest' anno si è lavorato molto nell' Anatomia, ed il Terenzii, ed il Fracassati, che vi hanno discorso sopra, hanno fatto bene la lor parte, ma non ci erano il Sig. Cav. Finchio, ed il Sig. Dott. Tommaso, che vuol dire assai. Ringrazio in fine V.S. delli attributi i che si compiace darmi, troppo superiori al vero; ma Ell' ha voluto mostrare la sua facondia, non meno che la sua cortesia. E mentre io Le ratifico sempre disposta la mia volontà per ogni sua occorrenza, resto augurandole intera prosperità.

In the year 1679 Anne Viscountess Conway died. Lord Conway was absent in Ireland, but "Baron Francis Mercury Van Helmont preserved her in her coffin above ground, in spirits of wine, having a glass over her face in order that her husband might see her before her interment[1]." In 1871 her coffin was in "Ragley Old Vault," Arrow Church, Warwickshire. Finch[2] writes to Conway consoling him, and adds:

I am for her sake to beg you to marry again for since it pleased God to take your only son a child to Heaven, to your own great name and family, to your person and virtues you owe a successor, which since my dear sister was now incapable of giving you, it may be God was pleased by calling her to your only offspring to make way for a more durable issue and to free her from a perpetual headache and as great a heartache in the prospect of seeing you childless....'Tis a debt due to her memory, who wished you a happy father, to the ashes of all your noble ancestors, and what you can never answer to God or man, if you endeavour not the satisfying of it by a speedy second marriage.

She had suffered from severe headache, night and day, which never left her, till her death. On one occasion she went to France in order that her cranium might be opened, but the French surgeons declined to undertake the operation, though they ventured to make incisions in the jugular arteries[3]. In the large collection of letters of Finch to his sister Anne[4] as far back as 1652 he constantly writes of her ill-health and gives her advice as to the care she should take of herself.

Baines writes[5] at the same time seconding Finch as to the marriage and gives advice which reveals at once his ideas on Eugenics:

...but as to this point I will revive in myself the dead name of a physician and speak to you as such, that none of us may miss our great intention that you might have an offspring. I wish you then a lady by no means tall, rather low, by no means very sanguine, especially red in her face, but rather inclined to pale, not of a fixed masculine consistency but of a feminine lax temper, by no means fat or indeed lean, but in the mediocrity, healthful as to herself and born of healthful and fruitful parents.

[1] *Miscellanea Genealogica et Heraldica*, 1890, 2nd series, vol. III, p. 3.
[2] *Calendar of State Papers—Domestic*, 1679-1680. 1679, Dec. 18-28. Pera of Constantinople.
[3] *D.N.B.* quoted from Ward, *Life of Henry More*, p. 206.   [4] Brit. Mus. *Addit. MSS.* 23215.
[5] *Calendar of State Papers—Domestic*, 1679-1680. 1679, Dec. 18-28 (?).

This is splendid advice in the giving, but surely rather difficult in the taking! The last clause sums up modern views to a large extent and certainly is the "common sense" view.

Baines seldom speaks of himself as a physician and only once have I seen him mentioned as prescribing medicine[1]. However, he had a pretty shrewd idea of the value of the "Imponderabilia" in the treatment of disease. Writing to Lord Chancellor Finch about somebody taking mineral waters, he adds, "...Again, my Lord, I speak not out of opinion but knowledge, that the meer opinion or conceit that a patient hath of his physitian that he is under, or physik he is in, does, of itselfe, reall cures...."

His views on "child-welfare," as it is now termed, are correct, but all his reasons for supporting them could not at the present day be justified. In the same letter he says:

My Lady Essex nursing her owne child, to me, my Lord, is a very gratefull story, showing good nature, great love to her husband, lack of pride or coyness, tender compassion and no aversion to care and pains. Sure I am there is less danger by it then in the frequent bearing of children, and by it she restamps her own good qualities upon her offspring.

Daniel Finch, writing to his uncle Sir John in 1680[2], gives his opinion of Baines' knowledge in medical matters and at the same time in a few words writes a justification of post mortem examinations. He tells how his last child died of convulsions, having lived two months only, and adds:

...I have sent you the observations of the doctors upon the dissecting of this last child that died, and entreat the favour of Sir Thomas Baines to peruse them, and *if?from them he can make any judgment for the preservation of them that remain* [the italics are my own] I do presume to premise myselfe that kindnesse from his charity as well as friendship.

In the present Book-room at Burley there are none of Sir John's volumes to be found, but an interesting folio Prayer Book which he gave to his sister-in-law. On the fly-leaf is written "Given unto Elizabeth Finch, August 28th Anno Domini 1650, By, Her Deare Brother Mr John Finch." This book passed to Elizabeth's son Daniel and for many years after was the family register of the births and deaths of Daniel's very numerous children. Francis Barnard's book of "Decumbitures[3]" testifies to the ill-health of these children. From the position of the stars at moment of onset of illness he thought himself capable of making a prognosis!

---

[1] *Calendar of State Papers—Domestic*, 1671–1672, p. 7. "1671, Dec. 2, Dublin. Sir G. Rawdon to Viscount Conway...concerning his wife's health and acknowledging a prescription procured from Dr Baines by his Lordship."

[2] *Finch Report* (Hist. MSS. Comm.), p. 78. May 10th, 1680.

[3] MS. in Library of Sir Wm. Osler, Bt. This volume is wrongly lettered on the binding "C. Barnard." By a comparison with MSS. of both F. and C. Barnard at the Brit. Mus. the handwriting is plainly that of Francis and not of Charles.

Francis Barnard (1627–1698) and Charles Barnard (1650–1711) were both sons of Rev. Samuel Barnard of Croydon. They both possessed fine libraries and, as seen by the catalogues of the sales, they had many books on Astrology. Francis was elected assistant-physician at St Bartholomew's Hospital in 1678, but even after this date, as seen from entries in Sir Wm. Osler's MS., he was still applying the results of Astrology to his medical work. He is represented by "Horoscope" in Garth's poem *Dispensary*. Charles, as shown by the Charterhouse Records, was appointed in June, 1679, "Surgeon of this Hospital" in the place of W. Nurse. Heneage Finch had recommended him to Charterhouse. He was also serjeant surgeon to Queen Anne, and was elected surgeon to St Bartholomew's in 1678.

Amongst the note-books found at Burley and sent to the Public Record Office is one, which has not previously been mentioned. It is a thick quarto volume and is in the writing of Baines and in Latin. It is chiefly "On Physick," but commences and closes with one of those very flowery and eulogistic letters that Finch and Baines were so fond of addressing to their Patron the Prince (*Princeps*) of Tuscany. This is followed by a treatise on the "Different Schools of Medicine," then begins the chief concern of the volume; a list of metallic and vegetable remedies, giving properties and indications as to their use, also a list of diseases and under the name of each its treatment is discussed. Everything is arranged in alphabetical order and is followed by a very lengthy index. The book therefore might well serve as a physician's "vade mecum." In the first section are "Alchymia," "Annihilatus Foetori," "Acetu," "Aqua" (all kinds), "Aurum," "Argentu" and "Antimonium."

From the letters and one of the note-books which were at Burley we may obtain an idea of the life of Finch and Baines in Turkey and it seems to have been very much as Baines had expected. There are accounts of interviews with the "Grand Signor" and various audiences with ministers and of discussions on numerous trade and political topics, but these last are not of very great interest. One remark of Finch's about the "treacherous Turk" in a letter to L. Hyde, April, 1677, must be quoted: "I wish the Peace of Poland may prove as honourable as is believed and given out to be. But I learn already that the Articles in Turkish are different from those in Polish, and given forth to all courts[1]."

Naturally from the importance of the station of Finch and Baines in Turkey there were a great many visitors to the Embassy and Finch quite often describes the arguments which were carried on throughout, or after dinner. In his note-book Finch sometimes gives the list of those present. The various ministers from other countries were heartily welcomed by Finch and Baines, and the

---
[1] Brit. Mus. *Addit. MSS.* 17017, f. 56.

door was by no means closed to the Jesuits. The reports of the conversations bring out the fact that they were very often on religious subjects and that some very sane remark was always to be expected from Sir Thomas. Finch is always careful to record Baines' opinions and seems to take great pride in his powers of argument and in what "T.B. replied." Covel tells of a discussion which Baines had on the Mahommedan Faith with one Vani Effendi. Baines recognized his own powers and gave his opponents time to consider their answers. "The Rector of the Jesuits dined with me, and brought with him another Jesuit, a learned man (both were French) being to answer an objection Sir Tho. Baines had made, and had given him three days for his reply [the discussion chiefly turned upon the definition of *una fides, unus baptismus et unus dominus*][1]."

They both held very strong opinions on the question of religious beliefs and Finch makes an interesting note on 21st–31st July, 1675, at Pera of Constantinople: "Mr Brown (the clerk) averred to Sir Thomas and me that Mr Chillingworth did in his sermon on the Resurrection speak words to this purpose 'that what advantage the resurrection of Christ brought to his living well he could not resolve.'" This idea must have appeared very heretical to dear Sir John and Sir Thomas.

In a discussion with the French Ambassador it was agreed that it was unwise to preach the doctrine of the Crucifixion to the Chinese, as in their eyes nobody but a criminal could have suffered that form of death. The French Minister felt strongly about this matter and "Begg'd deane of the Colledg of Cardinalla *de Propaganda fide* that they (Jesuits) might be enjoyned to preach Christ onely glorified." The amusing part was that a short time afterwards, perhaps made reminiscent with wine, the Frenchman began to relate some incidents of his early life in Paris. Baines was much shocked, leant forward, and in his quiet way "reply'd onely 'Et che dirà il Crucifisso.'" Finch states that "the Frenchman was struck dumbfounded and was filled with astonishment at so unexpected a glosse, which he sayd was a more efficacious sermon then he had heard from the Capuchin Fryers[2]."

Amongst the papers found at Burley and sent some years since to the Public Record Office were a number of loose manuscript sheets in the handwritings of Finch and Baines. Many of these deal entirely with Theological subjects and were often written on Sundays. Several are headed by a text from the New Testament and most of them, it must be admitted, make rather wearisome reading. Finch's page on "Descartes" may very well be one of the sheets of the "Treatise" which he sent weekly to his sister. One essay by Baines is entitled "How far Human Reason is exercised in the matter of Religion." It

[1] *Finch Report* (Hist. MSS. Comm.), vol. II, p. 133, extract from Finch's note-book, March 30th, 1676.
[2] *Ibid.* pp. 143 and 144.

is curious that Finch attempts to make Geometry the "hand-maid" of Theology and "the line A.B." is called in to aid in proving the truth of certain religious beliefs.

In a letter, 11–12th May, 1681[1], Baines congratulates the Earl of Conway on his becoming Secretary of State, and adds:

> I hope also I shall live to hear of these following things brought about by your Lordship's means. The taking away of coffee Houses....For indeed they are inconsistent with government. What Prince in the world suffers them? Nay the Grand Signor, in whose country it is their naturall drinke and governs with rods of iron, yet his irons would not be strong enough if Coffee Houses, these mints of mutiny, were suffered. In the second place reformation of Playhouses. How many men that want money for the necessary provisions of their own familys fool it away there?...The last thing my Lord is the luxury of clothes.

Baines considered that money should not be wasted on dress but invested in plate and jewels, in the stable, or rich furniture, as the investment would be so much more lasting.

Finch jotted down many curious things in his note-book and in January, 1677–8, he was told how to make coffee. This method of making the drink, I am informed, is a very good one. One cannot help thinking that the second brew "for ordinary people" might be used now to promote "war economy."

Jan. 15–25; 1677–78.

> Take Coffé and putt to it eight times its weight of water Then lett it boyl till it is conseumed one fourth. Then a little fayr water to it, and that precipitates it, and all the substance falls to the bottom. Then pour off the clear drinke into one or more recipienes and let it simper over the fire or stand warm, and so you have a choice Coffé all day for your friends. To the footes [*i.e.* coffee grounds] pour as much water as before, and boyl it till a third part be consumed, and then you have a coffé for ordinary people.

Another item given in the note-book is of great interest both historical and medical, for it tells of the death of "Madame," Henrietta Anne, Duchess of Orleans and fifth daughter of Charles I. She died very suddenly in 1670 and shortly after drinking some chicory water. Circumstances were such that poisoning was suspected and a post mortem examination was performed. Over the body Bossuet delivered one of his famous *Oraisons Funèbres*, in which he says "Madame se meurt, Madame est morte," and in which he does not state explicitly whether she died a natural death or not. The Comtesse de la Fayette discusses the circumstances of the death at great length, and Littré in his *Médecine et Médecins* deals with the same question. The truth seems to be that "Madame" died from the results of a perforating ulcer of the stomach and this is the view taken by a "chirurgien du Roi d'Angleterre[2]" who was present at the autopsy.

---

[1] *Finch Report* (Hist. MSS. Comm.), vol. II, p. 112.
[2] MSS. français, No. 17025, as cited by Littré.

Dr Norman Moore tells me that this is one of the first occasions on which the above lesion was noted post mortem. Here is the account given to Finch who writes on December 20–30th, 1675, saying:

...the new Bailo, L. F. Morosini, who had been ambassador in Savoy, France and Vienna, made me a return of my first visit...He told me for certain that there was a hole found in the stomach of Madame...as big as one's finger, and that he had not bin two hours from St Cloue, from the company of Madame before he heard the news of her death from the Dutchesse of Elboeuf, who treated him that night at supper.

The nephew Daniel Finch apparently made any necessary purchases for Finch in England; some of the orders throw light on the customs and tastes of the times: "Corks by all conveniences are necessary, and when you send any more wine, I pray forget not an adjunct of Northdown ale and a lesse quantity of Mum[1]." In the matter of clothes Finch was quite particular:

I desire you to send me out a summer suit, but take notice (?) that gravity of apparrell must not consist in any very (?) sad colours, for none here but Jewes wear them...I pray send me some scarlet and black ribband, and a piece or two also of some narrow ribband, twopenny broad...[2].

I have been unable to find any letters from Finch or Baines to Henry More, the man who exerted such an influence on both their lives, for he had had them under him when their minds were still plastic and so any mention of him is for that reason very interesting. As we have mentioned above, More several times wrote to Sir John at the direction of his hostess at Ragley. Baines, in the letter to Covel (p. 63), sends an interesting message to the Platonist:

To my Dear and Honour'd Tutor present me in all service and in most faithfull affection more particularly: I pray tell him he brought me up a scholler; but I have brought myselfe up a Merchant: and therefore look very near to the Exchanges I make *quid pro quo*: therefore I finding by our letters that when I quote Virgil he makes a return to me in a piece of Ovid: the trade is so disadvantageous that I must break it off. I Quote Austin He quotes Dod and Clever: Alas poor Merchant wither wilt thou goo....

As early as 1677 Finch wearied of the work at Constantinople and during this year he desired Conway to obtain a position for him in England and also wrote to the Lord Treasurer, the Earl of Danby (Sir Thomas Osburn). In the letter to Covel quoted in part above, Baines says that Finch had put himself in the Lord Chancellor's hands and would acquiesce in what he wished. This was in 1679, and by January, 1680–1, arrangements were being made to send out Lord Chandois to succeed Finch, but he did not arrive till June, 1681, and Finch did not leave until the autumn of that year.

[1] *Finch Report* (Hist. MSS. Comm.), vol. II, p. 65. The word "mum" is defined in the *Oxford Dictionary* as a "beer brewed in Brunswick."
[2] *Ibid.* p. 64.

CHAPTER IX

DEATH OF BAINES

Dr Thomas Allen, a Fellow of the Royal Society, was to act for Baines as Professor of Music at Gresham College whilst the latter was in Turkey, but in 1681, Wm. Perry was chosen to take Baines' place[1]; however, Baines died on the 5th September, and could not have heard of the change.

In August, 1681, Baines was stricken with his last illness, and the story could not be better told than in Finch's own words in his note-book and letters.

Memorandum by Sir John Finch, Aug. 28th, 1681.

My dearest friend, Sir Thomas Baines, now lying very sick and weak, I fearing his disease might prove mortall, with great sorrow of heart I told him my opinion of his condition, and desired him, whilst he was in perfect understanding, to tell me, since he had given me all his estate, both reall and personal, and made me his sole executor by his last will and testament, published June the second 1673: what he would have me dispose out of his estate and to whome. Whereupon, after many thoughts he desired, confirming and ratifying his will published in 1673, that what he should now further appoint and order might be annexed a codicill to the said will[2].

Then there follows a list of bequests to Baines' brothers, half-sister and nieces, also £50 for Henry More, with which he was to buy a ring, something for Edward Brown, clerk, Wm. Carpenter (Finch's secretary) and Zaccarias, Baines' "faithful Armenian servant."

A few days after the death of "honest Dr Baines" Finch wrote to his brother Heneage and on the same day made out the codicil to his own will, which is printed below (p. 81).

Dear brother, and most honoured Lord, I have lost Sir Thomas Baines, and your Lordship in him, and your family the faithfullest servant, as well as the best of friends, after fifteen days accession of a malignant feavor, added to the inexpressible torments of the stones in his bladder (for being open'd there were two, each as bigg as large walnutts): on Monday September the 5 at three of the clock in the afternoon, he gave up his soul into the hands of most mercifull God, and I received his last breath. There needs no comment to your Lordship upon this subject, who knew all things that ever passed between us, and have been exercised in griefs of a high nature. Though I am weak in bed yet I hold absolute necessity to write now, in regard that I would entreat your Lordship to be early in doing at the Prerogative office what is necessary, for I have no insight in probate of wills, and therefore I am glad it is under your Lordship's care, Sir Thomas his will is in your hands as my own, and Sir Eliab Harvey hath duplicates also, wherefore I send you not a copy of it, but the

---

[1] Ward, *Lives of the Professors of Gresham College*.   [2] *Finch Report*, vol. II, p. 117.

codicill now to Sir Thomas his will I send you a copy of: and so beseeching the Almighty to have your person and family in his holy protection, I rest with unspeakable affection, your dear brother and most humble and most obedient servant.
Postscript. My Lord, in this disorder of thoughts and weakness of body, I lye under, I had like to have forgotten to congratulate with your Lordship his Majesty's favour in creating you Earle of Nottingham, which now I doe from all the facultys of my soul, beseeching Almighty God to grant you a long and happy life[1].

Sir John Finch's note-book also contains some interesting items jotted down at this time:

...but that which cutt off the thread of all my worldly happinesse and application to business was the malignant double tertian which seised, August the 22nd my dear friend Sir Thomas Baines, and on Monday the 5th of September brought him to his last end...which irreparable losse brought my tertian to a double tertian also, and that reduced me to so much weaknesse that I was given over by my physitian, one Altios a Portugese Jew, and by all others especially upon my relapse.

I gave Mr Jenkins the chirurgeon and Mr Cranmer the ship surgeon each of them 28 zecchini for their pains in embalming him[2].

Finch's superstition has been remarked upon before, and looking back after Baines' death, he thought he discovered that the friends had been forewarned of the end of their conjoint life.

Two things I cannot omit. The first is that Sir Thomas and I sitting at table in our gallery at Pera, after supper, about a year before his death, there was a loud knocking upon the round table wee sat at, for near the space of a quarter of an hour. We called in three servants, my secretary, Derham, and Zacar, which last, astonished at the thing threw off the carpet [*i.e.* the table cover] and crept under the table; and then the knocking seemed to be above the table: as it seemed to us to be underneath it.

The second was that about foure dayes before Sir Thomas his sicknesse, one of my *dentes incisores* dropt out of my head without any pain whilst wee dined together; which seemes to confirm the interpretation of those who make the dreaming of the losse of a tooth to be the prediction of the losse of a friend.

About five days before his death, Sir Thomas told me that he was very certain he should dye, according to the method of providence: for that God had, under many diseases preserved him so long as he could be any wayes usefull or serviceable to me, but that now, returning into England where my friends were all so well in their severall posts, he could no longer be of any use to me, and therefore God would put a period to that life which he only wished for my sake.

Thus died the best friend the world ever had, for prudence, learning, integrity of life and affection; and I have many reasons (not to say demonstrations) to say that as he feared God, so God was in an extraordinary manner with him; but they are not so fitt to putt in paper, least the reall participation of God's spirit to him, even to revelations of things to come, might administer occasion of scoffing to those who scarce believe he hath not left behind him so great learning, accompanied with so great prudence and integrity of life.

"The Doctors" do not seem to have had very many intimate friends except the Conways, for practically all their lives were spent in foreign parts, and yet had Baines died at home, Finch could scarcely have felt the death of his friend

---

[1] *Finch Report* (Hist. MSS. Comm.), vol. II, p. 118. Sept. 9–19, Pera.
[2] *Ibid.* p. 162.

less hard to bear. Each was sufficient unto the other—in fact they were married to each other in all their interests—and we can picture Finch's great sorrow and grief when he realized that he could no more go to "Sir Thomas" for advice or for sympathy and consolation in "dark hours," that time when a true friend is a friend indeed.

Finch appeared in public as the leader of the two, but to what extent he was indebted to his helpmate and senior, Baines, for his success in diplomatic and scientific work, we shall never know. As we shall see, Finch was the last person in the world to withhold the credit due to Baines. One would like to have it so, and certainly one forms the idea in going through the letters and records, that "honest Dr Baines" was the guiding hand, the quiet worker behind the scenes, in Finch's career. Baines was not the man of action or of decision —this may be accounted for by his almost persistent ill-health; but the quiet, meditative and reflective natures, the profounder students, will ever fill a large place in the world. Ward[1] closes his sketch of Baines with the words "An instance of so long, intimate and inviolable friendship is very remarkable and but rarely to be found in history. And therefore he is very justly called by Dr Charlton 'fidissimus J. Finch Achates.'"

Finch wrote the rough draft in three pages of a document endorsed by himself "My dedication to Sir Thomas Baines[2]." There are no printed books by him in the catalogue of the British Museum, but in the dedication he mentions "the ensuing discourse" and it seems very probable that he intended to gather together those weekly essays which he used to send to the Conways. This document shows how intimate the friendship was of Finch and Baines, and we give it in full as it is a very remarkable record. It was certainly written after Baines was knighted and probably at "Pera of Constantinople," but the exact date is not known. A rough reckoning from the "internal evidence" of the MS. would suggest the date 1681.

Dedication by Sir John Finch to Sir Thomas Baines.

'Tis now full thirty-six[3] years since I began the happinesse of a uninterrupted friendship which the world never yet did equal, nor I believe will ever parallel. This alone might very well entitle you to this dedication, as a monument of our friendship. But though friendship is a thing sacred and coelestiall, yet I take gratitude to be a higher nature: for the first is a thing of choice, but the latter of perfect obligation: and upon this account of gratitude, I had rather entitle you to this address, that there might be nothing owing to me on your part, to whom I owe more than I can either acknowledge or return. For to speak to you Sir without flattery, a thing you have many years since taught me to abhorr, all that I doe or ever shall know, is deriv'd from those many hours of tendernesse of your regard for me made you throw away from your own most severe thoughts, which were in their relaxation and recreation

---

[1] Ward, *loc. cit.*   [2] *Finch Report* (Hist. MSS. Comm.), vol. II, p. 128.
[3] "Thirty-three" erased, "thirty-six" written over it.

more serious than those of many who passed as students, in the retirement of their closet. Those happy five years that in Christ Colledge in Cambridge gave me the advantage not onely of an education under so great a distinguisher of realitys from ayery notions, but also the freedome of an unreserved converse, make me blush that from so deep a foundation I have raised no higher a building. But at the same time it justly engaged me to submitt the errors of my fabrick to yourselfe, who are so great an architect in knowledge.

I must confesse that when your patience had in some measure fitted me to apprehend your discourses, I could not but profitt by them: and the small flights I tooke from the deductions they gave me, made me at last, wing'd with what you had taught, committ myselfe, like birds that leave their nests to the guidance of my owne strength and reason, which then became to you part of the delight, as before it was the whole trouble of our conversation.

Then it was we resolved upon a five years travel into Italy, where, after we had first spent one year in France, it pleased God to fix us upon our private.

In six and twenty years further intimate and endearing communication together (of which two-and-twenty were spent in Italy in our joint private study, and then our joint serving of Ferdinand the Second, the Great Duke of Tuscany of ever glorious memory, and wee never having bin separated two months from each other, but in the exercising of some kindnesse, though two and twenty of these years were spent in foreign parts, and eleven of them I was employed in his Majesty's service in Italy and Turkey), no wonder if our thoughts became so familiar to each other that sometimes wee forgott to whom they originally belonged ...especially on my part, who had the advantage of adopting those vigourous intellectual productions of yours: which is the third motive which makes me prefix the dear name of Sir Thomas Baines to the ensuing discourse for it is an act of justice to render back what I borrowed. Whatsoever therefore is agreeable in it to your solid judgment, call it yours, for I shall avow it to be so. What is not suitable to your thoughts, as several things may prove (for wee never esteemed difference in opinion to be a motive of making any difference in friendship), that must be mine, though it should not be so if I could thinke otherwise.

But lastly Sir when I consider that of the twenty-six years wee spent together since wee first left England, that wee never have bin separated two moneths from each other unlesse it were in the exercising some act of kindnesse though two and twenty of them spent in foreign parts: one half of them being employed in our private studys in Italy, and three years joint service of that prince of immortall prudence and memory, Ferdinand the Second, great Duke of Tuscany: the other half in the publick charges of recident in that court and ambassador to the Gran Signor, his Majesty my most gracious sovereign and master was pleased to confer upon my weake ability: your inimitable as well as unrequitable friendship though you were wracked with stone and tormented by the gout, inspiring you with courage to accompany me in your declining years and strength all this length of time and voyage: the greatest temporall blessing could have befallen me—so that I may say as truly of you as Aneas did Anchises, and I doe say more affectionately,

> Ille meum Comitatus iter maria omnia mecum
> Atque omnes Pelagique minas coelique ferebat
> Invalidus vires ultra sortemque Senectae.

When dear Sir I consider all this, I find that under all the ties of honour, friendship, gratitude and justice, you are entitled to this dedication...[*Unfinished Draft*].

Baines' body was embalmed at Constantinople, but the following "Epetaph on Sir Thomas Baines his Bowells inter'd att Constantinople made by Sir John Finch, 1682," as the manuscript at the British Museum[1] is endorsed, shows that the intestines were buried in Turkey, perhaps on "Demetrius Hill" whence

---

[1] *Sloane MSS.* 3329, ff. 5–6.

DEATH OF BAINES

Finch and Baines so often dated their letters, but Finch does not enlighten us on this point nor can I find any reference to it. It is not in the hand of Sir John Finch. Sir Edwin Pears, so long a resident in Constantinople, tells me that, with some friends, he made a copy of all the inscriptions in the English cemetery at Pera; unfortunately his MS. is deposited in the Chapel of the Embassy there and is now of course inaccessible! Sir Edwin Pears cannot recollect this particular epitaph. Such an epitaph, we think, is unique. We give it in the Latin of the period and also a translation.

>   Stupendæ, Piæ, ac omni Seculo Venerandæ Amicitiæ, S:
>   Inter
>   Clarissimum Illustrissimumque Virum
>   D: Thomam Baines Equitem Auratum
>   Cujus Interiora hic posita sunt;
>   Et
>   Illustrissimum Excellentissimumque D: Johannem Finch E: A: Legatum &c[ra]
>   Qui post suave et irruptum Animorum Connubium
>   Indivulsumque per XXXVI Integros Annos Sodalitium;
>   Has Exuvias Inenarrabili Amori Sacras,
>   Et sibi percharas Reliquias, Byzantinæ Ditioni
>   Gemebundus, Committit Simul et Invidet:
>   Quicquid præterea Pollincturâ condiri potuit,
>   Totum illud Secum abducit Legatus redux, in Angliam,
>   Charum sed Triste Consortium,
>   Ut eodem Sepulchro claudantur Inseparabiles Amici.
>   Nec enim par erat ut distinguerentur eorum Cineres mortui
>   Qui Mei ac Tui Nomina tanquam Amicitiæ Exosa et Infesta
>   Dum inter Vivos essent, in Exilium egerunt.
>   Atque hinc Amicitia quæ a cæteris Mortalibus pro nudo Nomine habetur,
>   Inter Nos indubitato extitit Res; ac vera Virtus;
>   Elapsis Seculis, licet Fabulosis inaudita, et futuris, ægrè imitabilis.
>   Decus hoc et honestamentum Amicitiæ, semper miraberis Viator; Sed modo deflebis
>   Si Viscera habeas vel Ferentis, vel Ponentis hoc Marmor.
>   Nunc de Integerrimo et Conjunctissimo Meo Bainesio, Pauca ex multis dicam.
>   In omni Re Literaria fuit tam profundè eruditus
>   Ut Platonis et Stagiritæ Manes in illo credideris redivivos
>   Nisi quod Sublimitate Ingenij Utrosque Illorum, Cæterosque omnes
>   Celebritate Nominis Insignes, facilè Superaret.
>   Momenta enim rationis Universalis Illi Soli (quod Sciam) inter Mortales innotuerunt.
>   Nec Minor fuit in Rebus gerendis: Quibus nominibus
>   Ss[ml] Ferd: II: et Cosm: III: MDH: Principes Immortalis Prudentiæ;
>   Bainesium Nostrum, inter Viros Summè præclaros annumerabant,
>   Famamque Ipsius, cum Colloquiorum, tum Literarum,
>   Insuper et Munerum frequentiâ extendebant:
>   More His Heroibus consueto, erga Viros Primarios.
>   Princepsque Pater, Illum Caput Ferreum Vocitabat:
>   Nam vel inter facetias (Vir enim fuit Amoenissimi Ingenij)
>   Nihil protulit quod non Simul in Scopum aliquem Serium dirigeretur.
>   Eâ denique illibata Virtute ac morum gravitate præditus fuit,
>   Ut nemo ausus sit Ipsius Aures Minus honestè dictis vulnerare.
>   Atroces Cruciatus; Exortos a Lancinatione Calculorum Vesicæ;

> Duo enim aderant In glandis Magnitudine,
> Christianâ fortitudine, ultrâ Stoicismi jactantiam pertulit.
> Tanti Viri, Talisque Amicitiæ irreparabilem proh dolor! Jacturam feci;
> Dum inter Amplexus et Gemitus, ultimum Ipsius Spiritum Exciperem;
> Die V: Septembris H: III. PM: MDCLXXXI: Æt: Suæ LIX.
> Vivam Charissimé! Memor Nostræ Amicitiæ, et
> Nulla Dies Unquam Memori Nos eximet Ævo.

This is erected to the wonderful, pious Friendship, to be venerated in every age, between the most renowned and illustrious man Sir Thomas Baines, Knight, whose bowels are deposited here, and the most honourable and excellent Sir John Finch, Knight, Ambassador, etc., Who after a beautiful and unbroken marriage of souls and a companionship undivided during XXXVI complete years, with groanings commits (and at the same time envies) these parts, sacred to an unspeakable love, and these remains very dear to him, to the Byzantine dominion: Whatever further of the body by preparation could be embalmed, all this the Ambassador brings with him coming home into England, a dear but sad companionship, so that the inseparable friends may be enclosed in the same tomb: for it does not appear right that their dead ashes should be distinguished who, whilst they were living put far away from them the words Mine and Thine, as hateful and hostile to friendship: and hence Friendship which to other mortals is a bare name, between us without doubt became a great thing, and a true virtue, in times gone by perhaps unheard of in history, and in the future scarcely to be imitated. This ornament and honour to friendship, always thou shalt wonder at oh traveller, but now thou shalt weep, if thou hast a heart like his who bears or like his who places this marble.

Now let me say a few things out of many, concerning my most honourable and beloved friend Baines.

In all things literary he was so profoundly learned that thou wouldst have believed the shades of Plato and the Stagirite to have lived again in him, were it not that he easily surpassed each of them in the sublimity of his knowledge, and all other famous men in the celebrity of his name: for to him alone (as I know) were known the movements of universal reason. Nor was he less great in what he did: on which account the most serene Ferdinand II and Cosimo III M.D.H. Princes of immortal wisdom, numbered our Baines amongst the most famous men, and spread forth his fame by conversations, letters, and above all by their gifts, as is the manner of these heroes towards remarkable men, and the Prince, the father, used to call him "The Iron Head." For indeed in his jests (for he was a man of charming wit) he put forth nothing that was not at the same time directed to some serious object. Thereupon by this unimpaired virtue and by the gravity of his manners he was revealed so that no one dared to wound his ears with speeches less becoming. Cruel tortures, arising from the laceration of the stones of the bladder (two were of the size of a walnut) he bore with Christian fortitude, beyond the boasting of the Stoicism—alas what grief! I have suffered the irreparable loss of such a man, and of such a friendship, whilst between embracing and groaning I have listened to his last breath on the Vth day of September IIIrd hour P.M. MDCLXXXI: in the LIXth year of his age.

I shall live, O beloved! mindful of our Friendship, and no day shall ever remove us from a remembering age.

CHAPTER X

RETURN OF FINCH

Finch came home to England on board the *Oxford* with the sad cargo of Baines' coffin and arrived at the Downs in July, 1682. He wrote his last will on this voyage and in the early part of the journey was evidently in very poor health. He visited Italy and wrote to his nephew on March 11th–21st, 1681–2: "...In this time I have been at Leghorn, I have here and from Florence furnished myself with the best sett of pictures, I dare say, that are in any private gentleman's hands. They are above sixty in number, and four of them of Carlo Dolce[1]." He intended to cross over France from Marseilles to Calais "by *lettica*" (horse-litter), but in the end came all the way by ship except that touching at Spain he made a short trip to Seville.

Sir John Finch, on his arrival in England in July, 1682, wished to defer the burial of his friend until the 5th of September, the anniversary of Baines' death[2], "and then I can say Nunc Dimittis Domine." He writes from the Downs 5th July, 1682, to Daniel Finch, telling of all the impedimenta which he brought back with him:

My last would tell you that I have resolved to go up the river by the *Oxford* and shall thinke myselfe extreamly happy to see [you?] at the long Reach. I believe a barge will be most convenient as I can put three or four trunkes upon it which cannot well be left for any other passage. Besides these there will be 53 trunkes more, and chests I brought from Constantinople 19 of which being books, are large and bulky and I have added to them 23 chests more of Italian pictures and statues; so that they will require a hoy or vessell that hath a dry hold to keepe them from rain above and sea water below there are also 15 chests Florence wine, a butt of Smyrna, 6 saragoza. If wine in bottles pay no custom, I will have 50 dozen bought for me with good corks. The bearer of this, Mr Peters, purser of the *Oxford*, who has been with me from Constantinople will acquaint you with some further particulars. I hope you and the Board will be satisfied with him as I have been....I am, blesse God, in much better health then I ever could have hoped after so much weaknesse and sicknesse and sorrow, and after so tedious a voyage[3].

I can find no evidence of the actual date of Baines' burial, nor any trace of a Latin oration which Finch is then said to have delivered. Peile, quoting the Audit Book of Christ's College, gives an interesting account of Finch's visit

---

[1] *Finch Report* (Hist. MSS. Comm.), vol. II, p. 167. March, 1681–2.
[2] *Ibid.* vol. II, p. 176, 1682, July 1–11, also see p. 121, letter of Finch to Daniel, 23rd Sep., 1681, O.S.
[3] *Ibid.* vol. II, p. 177.

to Cambridge; all the expenses are detailed, as the "Foundress' Chamber" was partially reconstructed by Grumbold for £9. 19s. 6d. and one end of the room wainscotted by Austin for £19. 12s.[1]. He was met by the Fellows and Scholars in coaches and on horseback at Trumpington, and men were drawn up at the College gate to welcome him. A dinner was given in his honour which cost £16. 17s. 3d. and wine at the dinner £2. 11s. 6d.

It is probable that at this time the scheme of the Finch and Baines Fellowship was discussed, for there is a letter from the Master (Cudworth) and Fellows to Finch dated 28th October, thanking him for the intended legacy and stating that Finch's nephew could be nominated the first Fellow. Peile gives a splendid account of this new Foundation which remained separate from the old one until 1860. The new Fellows were to be of any country, were not required to take Holy Orders, might "profess Physick, Law or Divinity" (but if in Orders, might hold with their Fellowship any preferment under £50), and those in the profession of Law or Physic might travel out of the kingdom for three years; for a longer or a second absence the permission of the College was required, but when in England they were required to be in residence. Any of the Founders' kin were to be preferred as Fellows "if well qualified with learning and manners." In his turn Daniel, second Earl of Nottingham, nominated seven Fellows, some of whom were members of the Finch family.

[1] "This work remains to the present day" (Peile), but I think the present Master has altered this room.

Plate VIII

Monument over the Grave of Finch and Baines, with Epitaph by Henry More (Christ's College)

EPITAPH ON THE MONUMENT OVER THE GRAVE OF FINCH AND BAINES.

EFFARE MARMOR,
Cuja sunt hæc duo quæ sustentas Capita
Duorum Amicissimorum, quibus Cor erat unum, unaq. Anima,
D. IOHANNIS FINCHII et D. THOMÆ BAINESII
Equitum Auratorum,
Virorum omnimodâ sapientiâ Aristotelicâ, Platonicâ,
Hippocraticâ
Rerumq. adeò gerundarum Peritiâ Planè summorum,
atq. hisce nominibus et ob præclarum immortalis amicitiæ
exemplum
sub amantissimi Tutoris HENRICI MORI auspicijs
hoc ipso in Collegio initæ
Per totum terrarum orbem celebratissimorum.
Hi mores, hæc studia, hic successus, genus verò
si quæris et necessitudines
Horum alter D. HENEAGII FINCHII Equitis Aurati Filius erat
HENEAGII vero FINCHII Comitis Nottingamiensis Frater,
Non magis Iuris quam Iustitiæ consulti,
Regiæ Majestati a consiliis secretioribus summiq.
Angliæ Cancellarii,
Viri prudentissimi, religiosissimi,
eloquentissimi, integerrimi,
Principi, Patriæ, atq. Ecclesiæ Anglicanæ charissimi,
Ingeniosâ, numerosâ, prosperâq. Prole præ cæteris
mortalibus, felicissimi :
Alter D. IOHANNIS FINCHII, viri omni laude
majoris Amicus intimus,
Perpetuusq. per triginta plus minus annos
Fortunarum ac consiliorum Particeps,
Longarumq. in exteras Nationes Itinerationum
indivulsus Comes ;
Hic igitur peregrè apud Turcas vitâ functus
est, nec prius tamen quàm alter
A serenissimo Rege Angliæ per Decennium Legatus
præclarè suo functus esset munere,
Tunc demum dilectissimus BAINESIUS suam et Amici
FINCHII simul Animam Byzantii efflavit,
Die V Septembris H. III. P.M. A.D. MDCLXXXI. Ætatis suæ LIX.
Quid igitur fecerit alterum hoc corpus animâ cassum rogas,
Ruit ; sed in amplexus alterius indoluit, ingemuit,
ubertim flevit
Totum in lacrymas, nisi nescio quæ communis utriq. Animæ
reliquiæ cohibuissent, Diffluxurum,

Nec tamen totus dolori sic indulsit nobilissimus
FINCHIUS,
Quin ipsi quæ incumberent solerter gesserit
confeceritq. negotia,
Et postquam ad Amici pollincturam quæ spectarent
curaverat
Visceraq. telluri Byzantinæ, addito marmore eleganter
a se pieq. inscripto, commiserat
Cunctasq. res suas sedulo paraverat ad reditum in
optatam Patriam,
Corpus etiam defuncti Amici a Constantinopoli usq.
(Triste sed pium officium) per longos Maris tractus
Novam subinde salo e lacrymis suis admiscens salsedinem
ad sacellum hoc deduxit.
Ubi funebri ipsum oratione adhibitâ mæstisq. sed
dulcisonis Threnodijs,
In Hypogæum tandem sub proxima Area situm
commune utriq. paratum hospitium solenniter
honorificeque condidit.
Hæc pia FINCHIUS officia defuncto Amico præstitit,
porroq. cum eo, in usus pios
Quater mille libras Anglicanas huic Christi Collegio
donavit
Ad duos socios totidemq. scholares in Collegio alendos
Et ad augendum libris quinquagenis reditum
Magistri annuum.
Cui rei ministrandæ riteq. finiendæ Londini
dum incumberet
Paucos post menses in morbum incidit Febriq. ac Pleuritide
Maximè verò Amici BAINESII desiderio adfectus et afflictus
Inter lacrymas luctus et amplexus charissimorum
diem obiit
Speq. beatæ immortalitatis plenus piè ac placidè in
Domino obdormivit
Die XVIII Novembris H. II. P. MN. A.D. MDCLXXXII. Ætatis suæ LVI.
Londinoq. huc delatus ab illustrissimo Domino D. FINCHIO
HENEAGII Comitis Nottingamiensis filio Primogenito
Aliisq. ejus filiis ac Necessariis comitantibus
Eodem in hoc sepulchro quo ejus Amicissimus heic conditus
jacet:
Ut Studia, Fortunas, Consilia, immo Animas vivi qui
miscuerant
Iidem suos defuncti sacros tandem miscerent cineres.

CHAPTER XI

FINCH'S DEATH, BURIAL AND WILL

Finch stayed at this time with his brother Heneage in London at "Queen-streete Howse" in Lincoln's Inn Fields, and here the last codicil to his will was written "October the last 1682." He did not for long survive the death of "T.B.," but died of pleurisy, 18th November, 1682.

The very next Audit in the book, referred to above, reads "charges at Trumpington when the coaches met Sir John Finch his corps," for the body was taken to Christ's College and buried with that of Baines as they had both so earnestly desired. A monument by Joseph Catterns of London was erected in the Chapel to the memory of Finch and Baines and stands between the organ chamber and the altar. The expenses were met by Daniel the second Earl of Nottingham and the monument was not completed before 1684. The pedestals bear a bust of Sir John Finch and Sir Thomas Baines and there is a long inscription (which is here reproduced, Plate VIII) composed by Henry More, who outlived his pupils by some years. The bodies are buried in front of the tomb and within the altar rails.

Finch and Baines have been further remembered at Christ's College. In 1882 they were among those chosen as "glass worthies" for two of the twenty-one lights of the west oriel window in the Hall, depicting the founders, benefactors and worthies of the College. The arms of Finch and Baines are correctly represented also.

Daniel Finch second Earl of Nottingham must have transferred Finch's pictures, books and papers to Burley-on-the-Hill when that house was completed about 1700. Besides the letters, note-books and pictures already described, a member of the Finch family has told me that there were a large number of anatomical and other medical and classical books, on the shelves of the "Long Library," which had belonged to Sir John Finch. No doubt some of these corresponded with those in the long list of books and MSS. which is to be found in one of Finch's note-books. Finch and Baines possessed a very good collection of medical books in Latin, Italian, Spanish and French. Harvey's book on the circulation of the blood is found wanting, but Finch had "Riolanus *de Motu Sanguinis*," "Vesali', *Anatomia*, Basileac 1543," and books by "Jul. Caes. Arant."

and by Fabricius ab Aquapendente. Amongst the English books Shakespeare is conspicuous by his absence. Boyle is represented by his *Experiments, Essayes,* and *Scepticall Chymist,* and Bacon by *Natural History, Opuscula* and *On Winds.* Quite properly we find Moore's *Philosophy* and "Sir K. Digby of *Plants.*" They also had "Mr Evelyn's *Sculpture"* and "Charleton's *Oeconomia,"* and for recreation *The Game of Chesse Play.* Unfortunately all these volumes were lost in a fire about ten years ago, but the letters, portraits and an official copy of the will were saved. The copy of the will still hangs in the East passage of the house and a photograph of it is reproduced (Plate IX). It is headed "On Board the Oxford January the 24th 1681–2," when Finch was bringing home Baines' body. It is very well illuminated in red and bears Finch's arms (Arg. a chevron bet. 3 gryphons passant sa.) quartering the arms of Fitzherbert with a crescent for cadency, a knight's helmet above with crest (a gryphon passant sa.) and mantling. The family of Finch was descended from the Fitzherberts.

IT HAVEING PLEASED GOD to reduce me to extreame weaknesse of body blessed bee his Name, he has continued mee in perfect soundnes of reason and Judgment I hold it necessary as a Christian not to leave my last Will and Testament to be made when it shall please God I shall draw towards my Departure. But beseeching the most merciful God who hateth nothing that he hath made through his mercy to purifye and wash mee from all my sinns through the blood of Attonement of Lord Jesus through whose Meritts alone I hope to be saved I render my Soule into the hands of the Greate and mercifull God Creatour of all things And my Body I commit to the Earth hopeing for a Joyfull Resurrection to be dispos'd of as follow's As also my Estate reall and personall according to such appointmᵗ. as hereafter I have made in this my last WILL.

IN THE FIRST PLACE I doe make and constitute my Deare and honour'd Brother HENEAGE LORD FINCH EARLE OF NOTTINGHAM LORD HIGH CHANCELLOUR OF ENGLAND my soule Executor Administratour and Assigne as the Law has constituted him my sole and proper Heire, Giveing and bequesthing unto him all my Estate reall and personall Except such part of it as shall by mee be dispos'd of in this my last Will and Testament Beseeching Almighty God to give him soe many Joy's and Comforts in this World that Hee may not have misse of or Sorrow for the losse of a Brother that so dearly and intirely loved him.

The Two Thousand pound I mentioned in a former Codicill to be added to Two Thousand more that Sir Thomas Baines has left and layd out as your Loᴾ my Executour shall thinke most advantagiously for the erecting Two Fellowshipps and Two Scollarshipps in Sir Thomas Baines his Name and Mine as also the applying of Fifty Pound per annum to the encrease of the Mastershipp of Christ College in Cambridge I doe ratify and confirm as also I doe appoint the paying to a farthing all the legacy's mentioned in Sir Thomas Baines his last Will to his Brothers Neeces and friends therein mention'd, desireing you to take notice that all the legacy's mention'd to be paid in Dollars are already by mee fully satisfy'd.

To my Nephew Charles Finch Fellow of All Soules Colledge in Oxford and to his Heires forever I doe give my Manor of Herald near Ipswich as an Evidence of the affection I have for him both as an Uncle and a Godfather.

To my Nephew Edward Finch Fellow of Christ Colledge in Cambridge and his Heirs I doe give my Parsonage of Ashford in County of Kent Beseeching God prosper him in all his Study's and Erect them to his Glory.

To my most Deare Nephew Daniel Lord Finch I give that Diamond Ring which is wound around with black thread or else such other as hee shall please of the whole number

of Rings leaving it to your owne Inclination to give whatsoever of my Estate Reall and Personall I have bequeth's unto you as you thinke fitt.

To my honour'd Neece My Lady Essex Finch I give and bequeth as a Testimony of my Respect such of the Saphire Rings as she shall be pleased to accept of, To my Deare Neece My Lady Mary Finch I give a payr of Diamond Braceletts that are made up onely of Dymonds and are worked something in the Fashion of snakes bones.

To my most dear and ever honour'd Lord Edward Conway one of his Maj$^{ty's}$ Principall Secretary of State I give and bequeth a Fascette Diamond of about Four Caratts in circe which accompany's another of the same bigness that was belonging to Sir Thomas, Beseeching God to prosper him in all his concern's. To my Dear and honour'd Tutor and Friend Dr Henry Moor I give Fifty Pounds to layd out in what hee likes best as a Memorial of my affection towards him.

To my Secretary William Carpenter in consideration of his faithfull Service I give the Summe of Three Hundred Pound Sterl-. intreating your Lo^p: my Executour for my sake to keepe him in your good Grace and Favour and advance him to such Charge as You find him most capable of, To Zacchar a faithfull Armenian Servant to Sir Thomas Baines I give the summe of Three Score Pounds sterling desiring your Lo^p: for both our Sakes that are deceas'd not to lett him a lively hood in England hee being soe warmly recommended to Mee to provide for by Sir Thomas.

My Body I have order'd if I dye at Sea to be embalm'd and putt into the same chest with that Sir Thomas Baines his Corps upon the consignment of which and such other goods as laden on board the Oxford of mine unto you or your Heire I doe order that one Hunder'd and Twenty Pound Sterling be presented to Captain Christopher Mason the Commander of that his Ma$^{ty's}$ Shipp, I doe bequeth Thirty Pound to be bestow'd amongst the Officers and Company of the said Shipp, I doe likewise desire your Lo^p: my dear Brother and Executour to cause my Body to be putt in one common Chest together with that Sir Thomas Baines his Corps and to be interr'd according to our Discretion in the Chapell of Christ Colledge Cambridge. I doe likewise order that Ten Pound Sterl: be given unto the Poor of Parish of St Andrew's in which Christ Colledge Lyeth and is scituated to be distributed in such Manner and forme as the Master and Fellows of Christ Colledge shall appoint.

And so my Dear and Honour'd Brother I give you my last Farewell Beseeching Almighty God the Creatour of all things through the Death and Attonement of the Lord Jesus Christ to give Us a joyfull Resurrection together in the last Day, where all Tears shall be wiped away from our Eyes through the Meritts of Jesus Christ whose Sorrow's purchased our Eternall Joyes as I hope and believe. GIVEN Under my hand this twentyfourth of January 1681-2 Aboard the Oxford which being past Cephalonia is now under Sayl for Messina whither God in Mercy send mee safe if it be his Blessed Will. That I may once more see your face the greatest Comfort this World could afford mee JOHN FINCH Sign'd and publish'd in the presence of WILLIAM CARPENTER, the mark of Zachariah Sedgwick;

...PERA SEPTEMBER 9-19th 1681...My most Dear Brother and most honour'd Lord It pleased Almighty God to take Sir Thomas Baines to himselfe I haveing receiv'd his last Breath Monday the Fifth of September at three of the Clocke in the afternoon and since the good hand of God hath laid correction on mee besides the irreparable losse of Sir Thomas Baines by sending mee a double Tertian accompany'd with malignity. I have much reason to feare I shall never see your face and therefore according to my promise made to Sir Thomas Baines I by this Codicill to my Will made June the second 1673 Doe order and appoint that Two Thousand pounds sterling out of my Estate bee added to Two Thousand pounds out of Sir Thomas his Estate and the whole Four Thousand pounds Sterling be so layd out for the sole use and advantage of the Master and Fellow's of Christ. My Intentions were to buy lands and encrease the Mastershipp 50£ per annum and erect two Fellowshipps of 60 pounds per annum each and two Scollarshipps of Tenn pounds each per annum, but your Lo^{ps} Prudence Act by Advice with the Master and Fellows if I see you noe more as you please.

Sir Thomas and I desire to be bury'd in Christ Coll': Chappell and Hee is embalmed to that end and I have order'd my embalming also in case I rise not from my Bed of Sicknesse For the Mercy of God cause both these our Codicills to bee putt in Execution JOHN FINCH Signed and published in the presence of us William Carpenter, The marcke of Zachariah Sedgwick.

I SIR JOHN FINCH KNT haveing already made my Will and haveing there dispos'd of my Estate according to my entire satisfaction Doe upon a second perusall ratifye and agree with every part of it Unlesse in the particulars following First I appoint my Mannor of Herald in the County of Suffolke to be given wholly and solely unto my Dear Godson Charles Finch Fellow of All Soules in Oxford and his Heirs for ever Secondly To my Nepew Robert Finch I give all the Right Title and Profitts that may arise from my Parsonage in the County of Kent, Thirdly In regard that the paines of my Secretary William Carpenter in soe many years haveing been very great and being perform'd in Barbarous Country's very dangerous also I doe desire that he may receive the summe of Three hundred pounds Sterling as a reward on my part in some measure to his Labours and because Zaccar the Armenian Servant ought to be requited I doe order him One hunder'd pounds Sterling Beseeching your good Lo^p: my deare Brother to cause these Summes forthwith be paid and to take them both into your Lo^{p's}: particular Care and Protection being beyond all the money I have left them: Queenstreete Howse October the last 1682 JOHN FINCH...Signed and publish'd in the presence of us WILLIAM CARPENTER, The marke of ZACHARIAH SEDGWICK.

APPENDIX

THE "TABULAE HARVEIANAE"

Just before returning to France in May, 1916, I was lucky enough to find the Italian letter (p. 36) from Sir John Finch, in which he mentions the "Tavole," and it occurred to me that the anatomical tables, traditionally described as Harvey's (p. 7), should perhaps be attributed to Finch. I puzzled much over this question and early in August wrote to the Librarian of the Royal College of Physicians to learn all that was definitely known about these six anatomical tables. I was much interested in reading the Harveian Oration (see *British Medical Journal*, 28th October, 1916) to see that Sir Thomas Barlow, Bt., had arrived at a similar conclusion as to the *provenance* of the "tabulae," although by a different method of reasoning. I am indebted to Sir Thomas Barlow for some further notes on the question and these I have put together with my own.

There is no writing with the specimens nor marks on them to prove that they belonged to Harvey, but in presenting them to the College in 1823 the Earl of Winchilsea said: "I have in my possession some anatomical preparations which belonged to the late Dr Harvey." This was quite a natural mistake for Winchilsea to make, as Harvey's connection by marriage with the Finch family was well known to him, and even to this day the family have remembered Sir John Finch chiefly for his diplomatic career, losing sight of the fact that he was also a student of natural science and professor of anatomy. Let us suppose that the Tables did belong to Harvey. Why then did he leave such valuable specimens to the Finch family and not directly to the College which was his constant interest during his lifetime and to which he made such liberal gifts? The Tables are not even mentioned in his will. Sir John Finch left England in 1651 to study medicine in Italy and did not return till 1660, three years after Harvey's death, and it seems most unlikely that Harvey left such specimens to one who was so far away from him and yet made no entry of such a bequest in his will. Nor is it likely that Harvey left the "tabulae" to a member of the laity such as his niece Elizabeth (Sir John Finch's sister-in-law) or to another non-medical member of the Finch family.

It has been stated that Harvey made use of these "tabulae" at his lectures, but I am assured that he makes no mention of them in his *Praelectiones*. Besides,

APPENDIX

Evelyn tells us in his *Diary* that he (Evelyn) procured certain tables of anatomical specimens from Veslingius' assistant at Padua, and these Sir Charles Scarborough (intimate friend of Harvey and his successor as Lumleian Lecturer) thought unique throughout the world and borrowed for his own lectures.

> Nov. 5th 1652. Dr Scarborough was instant with me to give the Tables of Veins and Arteries to the Colledge of Physitians, pretending he would not onely reade upon them, but celebrate my curiositie as being the first who caus'd them to be compleated in that manner, and with that cost; but I was not so willing yet to part with them, as to lend them to the Colledge during their anatomical lectures, which I did accordingly.

Now had Harvey used such "tables" Scarborough would scarcely have considered them such rarities. As Sir Thomas Barlow says in a letter to me, "the conclusion from this that Harvey had no such tables at his lectures is, I think, morally certain." Evelyn gave his specimens, not to the College as Scarborough suggested, but to the Royal Society and at present they are in the Museum of the Royal College of Surgeons.

Thus I think it is most highly improbable that Dr Harvey ever had such specimens, and still more so that they were taken to Burley-on-the-Hill forty-three years after his death, when the present house was built in 1700. On the other hand, Sir John Finch must have been quite familiar with like anatomical preparations even when he studied anatomy at Padua and, after having been professor of anatomy at Pisa for some years, he makes his trip to Holland with the express purpose of investigating the method of preserving bodies and writes to his patron, Prince Leopold (pp. 35 and 36), comparing those he saw there with their own at Florence. Further, we know that some years after the death of Sir John Finch, his favourite nephew Daniel took with him to Burley his uncle's belongings even down to the most insignificant papers. The Earl of Nottingham's inventory of these things existed a few years ago, but at the moment I am unable to trace it.

We know definitely, then, that Finch had anatomical tables and we know that, more than one hundred years after his personal property was taken to Burley-on-the-Hill, such a collection was found there. It is not known that Harvey possessed these "tabulae" and I have shown that such a possibility is most unlikely.

INDEX

Academy of Sciences, Paris, 22
Accademia del Cimento, 22 *et seq.*, 28
Adrianople, 60, 62
Algiers, 45, 46
Allen, S., 33
—— Sir Thomas, 71
Altios, 72
Ambassadors, 58
America, 56 *et seq.*
Anatomy, 15, 16, 19, 23, 26, 36, 41 *note*, 42, 65
Andrich, 5, 18
Anne, Queen of Great Britain, 67
Aqueducts of Solyman, 62
Aquinas, tomb of, 11
Arabia, 62
Arantius, Julius Caesar, 79
Aristotle, 53, 75, 76
Arlington, Earl of, 45, 54 *et seq.*, 56, 59
Aselli, 23
Ashford, Parsonage of, 80, 82
Ashley, Lord, 54 *et seq.*
Ashmole, Elias, 32
Astrology, 2, 66 *et seq.*
Auberius, 23
Aubriet, Claudio, 23
Austin, 78
—— Samuel, 70

Backwell, Alderman, 39
Bacon, 80
Baines, Francis, 1
—— Richard, 1
—— Sir Thomas, birth of, 1; at school at Stortford, 1; takes degrees at Cambridge, 1; poem of, in praise of Molinetti, 13 *et seq.*; devotion to Sir John Finch, 17; arms of, 19; goes to Pisa, 22; suffered from paralysis agitans, 24; appointed professor of music at Gresham College, 30; advice to Daniel Finch, 33; counsels Sir John Finch as to marriage, 33; allowed to leave Gresham College, 39, 61; philosophy of, 43; not knighted until 1673, 44, 57; trip with Daniel Finch, 49; sends presents to Anne Viscountess Conway, 50; suffers from stone, and ill-health of, 51, 56, 57, 75; not appointed a Commissioner to New England, 56; letter to Anne Viscountess Conway, 57; the physician, 66; skilful in argument, 68; denounces coffee-houses, extravagance, and luxury, 69; jokes about Henry More in a letter, 70; successor of, at Gresham College, 70; death of, 71; Sir John Finch's epitaph over bowels of, 74 *et seq.*; burial of, 77; bequests of, 80 *et seq.*; *see also* Finch and Baines

Baldinucci, Filippo, *quoted* 52
Balliol College, 2
Barbarino, Cardinal, 50
Barbary, 46
Bargrave, John, 17
Barlow, Sir Thomas, Bt, 83 *et seq.*
Barnard, Charles, 66 *et seq.*
—— Francis, 2, 66 *et seq.*
—— Samuel, 67
Bate, George, M.D., 32
Bellini, Lorenzo, 23
Benedictines, the, 25
Bezar, lapis, 6 *note*
Bilsius, *or* Bils, Louis De, 35 *note*
Bilzio, 35
Bologna, 11
Bonfigliuoli, Silvestro, 23
Borelli, 22, 24, 41
Bossuet, 69
Boyle, the family of, 52
—— the Honourable Robert, *quoted* 34 *et seq.*; works of, 80
—— Roger Broghill, eldest son of the first Earl of Orrery, 50
Bridgewater Gallery, 21
Broghill, 50, 52
Broghim (?), John, 52
Bromley, Thomas, 64
Brown, Edward, 71
—— Henry, 24, 37, 68
Browne, Edward, 19
—— Sir Thomas, 19
Buckingham, George Villiers, second Duke of, 32
Burleigh House, Stamford, 53
Burley-on-the-Hill, Rutland, formerly seat of Earls of Winchilsea and Nottingham, 1; fire at, 7, 80; "tabulae Harveianae" at, 7, 83, 84; portraits of Finch and Baines at, 20, 51 *et seq.*; note-books, letters, and papers of Finch and Baines at, 27, 32, 40, 53, 61, 67, 68; present house built about 1700, 51, 79, 84; family register in folio prayer-book at, 66; library of Finch and Baines formerly at, 79
Butler, 11

Calais, 77
Calvin, John, 7, 8
Cambridge, 1, 11, 34, 39, 48, 63, 74, 77; *see also* Christ's College
—— Platonists, 1, 4, 48
Candia, 61
Capuchin Friars, 68
Carpenter, William, 60, 71, 81 *et seq.*
Carr, Doctor, 31
Carthusians, the, 6

11—3

86 INDEX

Cartwright, William, poems of, 4
Catharine of Braganza, Queen Consort, paintings presented to, by Sir John Finch, 52
Centurion, the, voyage of, 58
Chalon, Notre Dame of, 6
Chandois, Lord, succeeds Sir John Finch at Constantinople, 70
Charles I, 69
——— II, 30 *et seq.*, 34, 44, 47, 49, 54, 56, 57, 74; painting presented to, by Sir John Finch, 52
Charleton, Doctor, 73, 80
Charterhouse, 67
Chemistry, 41
Chester, 33
Chillingworth, Mr, 68
Chimacam, the, 61
Chimentelli, Valerio, 26
Chinese, missionaries to the, 68
Christ, pictures of, 51, 53
Christianity, 48, 49
Christ's College, 1, 31, 39, 62; Finch and Baines meet at, 3; Finch and Baines visit Henry More at, 56; life of Finch and Baines at, referred to, 74; burial of Baines at, 77; decorated for visit of Finch, Finch and Baines Fellowship at, 1, 78, 80 *et seq.*; burial of Finch at, and monuments to Finch and Baines at, 79
Civil War, the, 2
Clarendon, Edward Hyde, Earl of, 31
Clark, Sir Andrew, 44
——— Rev. Andrew, 2
Clement IX, 50, 55
Clever, 70
Clifford, Robert, 25
——— Sir Thomas, 25
Coffee, receipt for, 69
Collins, Richard, 18
Constantinople, 37, 38, 45, 54, 56, 57, 59, 70, 77; Sir John Finch at, 61 *et seq.*; epitaph over bowels of Sir Thomas Baines at, 74
Conway, Edward Viscount, afterwards Earl of, 5, 10, 30, 45, 50, 54, 58, 59, 62, 64, 70, 81; becomes Secretary of State, 69
——— Anne Viscountess, 3, 5, 6, 7, 9, 10, 34, 49, 62; letters from Henry More, 15, 43, 44, 48, 56; portrait by S. Van Hoogstraaten of (?), 21; poems addressed to, 48; letters to Henry More, 39; ill-health of, 7, 10, 11, 50, 59, 63, 65; turns Quaker, 63 *et seq.*; death of, 63
Cooper, Joseph, 64
Cornelio, Tommaso, 41
Cosimo III, Grand Duke of Tuscany, 64, 75
Covel, John, later Master of Christ's College, 62, 63, 68, 70
Cranmer, Mr, 72
Crellius, 43
Croker, Hon. John Wilson, 15
Croome, William, M.D., 32
Crossley, James, 39 *note,* 48
Cudworth, Ralph, Master of Christ's College, 78
Cust, Lionel, 21, 52 *et seq.*
Cypher letters, 38, 45, 51, 54 *et seq.*
Cyprus, 62

Danby, Earl of, 70; *see also* Osburn, Sir Thomas
Darwin, Sir George, 18

David with Goliath's Head, 52
Decumbitures, Francis Barnard's book of, 66
De Hooche, Peter, 21
Derham, 72
Descartes, 13, 41, 43, 68
Digby, Sir Kenelm, 5, 7, 11, 32; "powder of sympathy" of, 28; works of, 80
Dispensary, Garth's, 67
Dod, Henry (?), 70
Dolci, Carlo, 51 *et seq.*, 77
Donne, *quoted* 63
Dover, 59
Dresden, 52
Dryden, John, 32
Dunkirk, sale of, 39

Elboeuf, Duchess of, 70
England, trade relations of, 46, 62
Euclid, 53
Eugenics, 65
Evelyn, John, 32, 84; works of, 80
Exeter, Marquis of, 53

Fabricius, ab Aquapendente, 13, 15, 80
Fabroni, *quoted* 22, 24
Fallopius, 13
Fava, Doctor, 52; *see also* Baines, Sir Thomas
Fellowships of Finch and Baines at Christ's College, 78, 80 *et seq.*
Ferdinand II, Grand Duke of Tuscany, 26, 32, 34, 35 *note,* 40, 41, 45, 46, 50, 53, 64, 74, 75; patron of science, 22 *et seq.*; death of, 55
Finch, Anne Viscountess Conway,' 3; *see* Conway
——— Colonel Charles, 42
——— Charles, 80, 82
——— Daniel, later second Earl of Nottingham and sixth Earl of Winchilsea, 32, 33, 44, 59, 70, 77, 78, 79, 80, 84; goes to Italy, 46; builds present house at Burley-on-the-Hill, 51, 79, 84; marriage of, 57; children of, 66
——— Edward, 80
——— Lady Elizabeth, 7, 47, 66, 83
——— Lady Essex, 57, 66, 81
——— Francis, 2, 4, 5, 7
——— Sir Heneage, Recorder of the City of London, 1, 2, 3
——— Heneage, second Earl of Winchilsea; *see* Winchilsea
——— Heneage, Lord Chancellor, afterwards first Earl of Nottingham, 1, 3, 7, 32, 33, 43, 44, 47, 51, 54, 56, 57, 67, 70, 71, 79, 80; created Earl of Nottingham, 72
——— Sir John, birth of, 2; educated at Eton and Oxford, 2; horoscope of, 2; admitted to Inner Temple, 2; Oxford and Cambridge degrees of, 3; book dedicated to, 4; affection for his sister Anne Conway, 6, 20 *et seq.*, 59, 63; ill-health of, 6, 17, 51; letters to Anne Conway, 6, 12, 50; letter to Anne Conway about Quakers, 63; opinion of Van Helmont's Universal Medicine, 10, 11; refuses to be Consul of the English nation at Padua University, 11; "philosophical discourses" of, 12, 13, 73; ideas on plant physiology, 12; criticism of Descartes, 13; his account of circulation of the blood, 15 *et seq.*; Pro-Rector

INDEX

and Syndic of University of Padua, 17; arms of, 18 et seq., 80; professor of anatomy at University of Pisa, 22, 23, 42; English Resident at Florence, 24, 44 et seq.; acts as confessor, 25; physician to Queen of England, 26; epigrams on, 26 et seq.; knighted, 30; in love, 33 et seq.; interest in perception of colours, 34 et seq.; letters from Henry Oldenburgh, 32, 61; his house in Kensington later part of Kensington Palace, 32, 44; letters to Prince Leopold of Tuscany, 35 et seq., 41 et seq.; anatomical tables of, 36, 83 et seq.; trade disputes at Florence, 45; praised by Winchilsea, 47; letter to Anne Conway on friendship, 49; questions of Italians saluting English ships, 50 et seq.; presents paintings to Charles II and his Queen, 52; buys pictures in Italy, 52 et seq., 77; to enter politics in England, 54 et seq.; does not wish to go to Turkey, 55; on Council for Plantations, 56; appointed ambassador at Constantinople, 56, 61; chaplain of, 58; liberality of, 58; to make enquiries for Royal Society, 61 et seq.; letter from Prince Leopold of Tuscany, 64; a method of making coffee, 69; weary of Turkey, 70; writes of death of Baines, 71 et seq.; epitaph over Baines' bowels written by, 74 et seq.; return to England with Baines' body, 77; death of, and burial at Christ's College, 79; will of, 80 et seq.; see also Finch and Baines
Finch, and Baines, portraits of, 1, 20 et seq., 51 et seq.; note-books of, 1, 27 et seq., 53, 67, 72; Fellows of the Royal Society, 1, 32; Fellows of the Royal College of Physicians, 1, 30; benefactors of Christ's College, 1, 78, 80 et seq.; pupils of Henry More, 3; meet at Christ's College, 3; poems and songs of, 4, 47; set out for France, 5; arrival in Padua, 10; trip to Milan and Bologna, 11; superstitions of, 11, 28, 72; praised by Bargrave, 17; wreaths and monuments to, at Padua, 18 et seq.; take medical degree at Padua, 19; send dogs to Anne Conway, 19 et seq.; studies and experiments in physiology, chemistry, and pharmacology, 24, 27, 28 et seq., 41, 60; return to England, 30, 56; receive degree of M.D. at Cambridge, 31; visit to Holland, 34 et seq.; poor correspondents, 37, 40, 43; return to Florence, 39; visit Rome and Naples, 40 et seq.; library of, 41, 58, 77, 79; interest in serpents, 41 et seq.; Daniel Finch under care of, 46 et seq.; visit Henry More, 56; voyage to Turkey, 58 et seq.; life in Turkey, 58, 67, 70; investigate method of staunching blood, 59 et seq.; visit Malta, 60; interest in religion and theology, 62, 68; trip to Adrianople in interest of trade, 62 et seq.; advise Conway to marry again, 65; letter about wills of, 71; dedication of Finch to Baines, 73 et seq.; Fellowship of, at Christ's College, 78; tomb of, and epitaph, 79
—— Lady Mary, 81
—— Sir Moyle, 49
—— Pearl, 51
Finch-Hatton, George William, tenth Earl of Winchilsea; see Winchilsea
Finckio, Giovanni, 23; see also Finch, Sir John
Fitzherbert, arms and family of, 80

Florence, 46, 57, 59, 77, 84
—— Archbishop of, 51
Forbes, Tommaso, 28; see also Baines, Sir Thomas
Foster, Joseph, 2
Foxcroft, George, 48 et seq.
—— Mrs, 48, 56
Fracassati, Carlo, 23, 26, 27, 65
France, 5 et seq., 39, 59, 74, 77
—— Henry IV, King of, 7
—— Louis XIV, King of, 59

Galen, 16
Galileo, 23
Garth, Samuel, 67
Gascoigne, Sir Bernard, 25, 44
Geisufius, Samuel, 18
Gell, Mr, 1, 3
Geneva, 6, 8, 17, 57
Genoa, 46, 59
Geometry, 69
George IV, 52
Glanville, Joseph, 4
Gorges, Ferdinand, 57
Gostlin, John, 31
Gran Signor, the, Mahomet IV, 57 et seq., 61, 67, 74
Grantham, 34
Greatrakes, Valentine, 50
Greek Church, 58
Gresham College, 32, 44, 61, 71
Grumbold, 78

Hague, Treaty at The, 55
Hartlib, S., 31
Harvey, Sir Daniel, 7, 47, 56, 62
—— Sir Eliab, 7, 30, 71
—— Elizabeth; see Finch, Lady Elizabeth
—— Mrs, portrait of at Burley-on-the-Hill, 7
—— William, 1, 8, 12, 16, 22, 23, 28, 30, 47, 79; connection with Finch family and portrait of at Burley-on-the-Hill, 7; "tabulae Harveianae," 7, 83 et seq.; strange story about, 7; will of, 7
Henrietta Anne, Duchess of Orleans—"Madame," death of, 69 et seq.
Henry IV, King of France, 7
Herald, Manor of, 80, 82
Herodias, Carlo Dolci's painting of, 52
Hickman, Sir William, 56
Highmore, antrum of, 13
Hippocrates, 23, 53
Holland, 34, 46, 84
"Horoscope" in Garth's *Dispensary*, 67
Hospitals of France, 6
Hubbard, Captain, 50
Hunter, John, 24
Hyde, L., 67

Imponderabilia in medicine, 66
Ingoldsby, living of, 48
Inner Temple, 2, 56, 57, 59
Ipswich, Manor of Herald at, 80, 82

James II, 52
Janckenius, Otto, 10
Jenkins, Mr, 72
Jesuits, 68

INDEX

Jesus College, 48
Jews, 8, 58, 63, 70, 72

Keith, George, 64
Kensington Palace, 32, 44
Knolles, *quoted* 61

Lacteals, 23
La Fayette, Comtesse de, 69
Legh, Mr, 1
Leghorn (Livorno), 45, 46, 49, 55, 56, 57, 59, 60, 63, 77
Leopold, Prince of Tuscany, 22, 67; letters from Sir John Finch to, 35 *et seq.*, 41 *et seq.*, 84; letters from, 40, 64
Levant Company, 62
Lindisy, Henry, 18
Littré, 69
Lloyd, Charles, 64
London, Paris compared with, 6
Lorenzinus, Laurence, 26
Louis XIV, 59
Lumleian Lectures, 15, 84

"Madame" (Henrietta Anne Duchess of Orleans), death of, 69
Madras (Fort George), 49
Maestricht, 34 *et seq.*
Mahomet IV, 61
Mahommedanism, 62, 68
Maidstone, Lord, 54
Maine, 57
Malpighi, Marcellus, 15, 22, 23, 24
Malta, 60
Mary Magdalene, Carlo Dolci's painting of, 52
Mason, Captain Christopher, 81
Massachusetts, 57
Massereen, Lord, 33
Mattias, Prince of Tuscany, 64
Médecine et Médecins, 69
Medici, Princes of, 23, 31
Medicine, 26, 67
Melancholy, the, of Sir John Finch, 48
Mercator, 40
Merchettis, Domenico de, 19
——— Pietro de, 19
Mignet, Father, 6
Milan, 11
Molinetti, 4, 13, 17
Montpellier, 19
Montreuil, 59
Moore, Norman, 19, 70
Moray, Sir Robert, 32
More, Henry, 1, 3, 9, 13, 31, 50, 63, 70, 71, 80, 81; letters to Anne Viscountess Conway, 15, 34, 43, 48, 56; letters from Anne Viscountess Conway, 39 *note*; his epitaph on tomb of Finch and Baines, 79
Moretus, 10
Morice, Secretary of State, 54
Morosini, L. F., 70
Moyen, Cardinal, 7
——— College, 7

Naples, 49
Newbury, battle of, 2

New England, 57
Newton, arms of, 19
Norris, 2
North, life of, *quoted* 63
Nottingham, Earls of; *see* Finch
Nurse, W., 67

Oldenburgh, Henry, 32, 61
Oliva, 27
O'Neale, 54
Oraisons Funèbres, 69
Orrery, Earl of, 50; *see also* Boyle
Osburn, Sir Thomas, 57; *see also* Danby
Osler, Sir William, Bt, 2, 66 *note*
Ottoman Empire, 61
Ovid, 70
Oxford, 2
Oxford, the, 77

Padua, 10, 84; anatomical theatre at, 15; Pro-Rectors and Syndics at University of, 17 *et seq.*; British Syndics at, 18; monuments to Englishmen at, 18
Paris, 5, 6, 59 *et seq.*
Patrizi, Marchese, 41 *et seq.*
Pears, Sir Edwin, 75
Pecquet, 41
Peile, John, Master of Christ's College, 1 *note*, 19, 77
Penn, William, 64
Pepys, 15, *quoted* 44
Pera, 75
Perry, William, 71
Peters, Mr, 77
Petty, William, 30, 32
Pisa, University of, 22 *et seq.*, 84
Plague, the, 35, 63
Plantations, Council for, 56
Plato, 53, 75 *et seq.*
Platonists, the Cambridge, 4, 48
Pliny, 23
Poland, 61, 67
Pope, the; *see* Clement IX
Post-mortems, 66, 69
Potts, Mr, 3

Quacks, 50

Ragley, in Warwickshire, 3, 10, 32, 33, 48, 57, 58, 64, 65, 70
Ravilliac, 7
Rawdon, Sir George, 50, 66 *note*
Red Sea, enquiries as to, 62
Redi, Francesco, 25
Religion, the Mahommedan, 62
Ricci, Cardinal Michel Angelo, 40 *et seq.*
Rich, Lady Essex; *see* Finch, Lady Essex
Riolanus, *de Motu Sanguinis*, 79
Rome, 41 *et seq.*, 49 *et seq.*
Rouen, 5
Royal College of Physicians, 1, 39, 83 *et seq.*
——— College of Surgeons, museum of, 84
——— Society, 1, 22, 31, 32, 61 *et seq.*, 71
Rusma, enquiries as to, 62
Rust, Dr George, 4
Rusthall, 33
Rutland, 1

INDEX

Rycaut, Paul, 61 *note*
Rye, 5

St Bartholomew's Hospital, 67
St John, Order of, 60
Scarborough, Sir Charles, 84
Selden, 4 *note*
Serpents, grotto of, 41 *et seq.*
Servetus, Michael, 8
Severino, M. Aurelio, 41
Seville, 77
Shakespeare, 80
Shipley, A. E., Master of Christ's College, 31, 78 *note*
Skene, Giles, 64
Smyrna, 60, 63
Socinians, the, 43
Socinus, 8
Spain, 77
Stamford, 53
Steno, Nicholaus, 23, 26
Stokeham, William, 18
Stortford, 1
Sybaticus, 17
Sylvester, Mr, school of, at Oxford, 2

"Tabulae Harveianae," the, 7, 83 *et seq.*
Talbot, Sir Gilbert, 28
Targioni-Tozzetti, Giovanni, 52, *quoted* 25 *et seq.*, 42, 64
Taylor, Jeremy, 4
Terenzii, 65
Thomas Aquinas, tomb of, 11
Timoni, Emmanuel, 18
Tompson, Thomas, 18
Torpedo-fish, 24
Tructwyn, Tilmann, 23 *et seq.*, 42; epigram and epitaph of, 25
Trumpington, 78
Truttwyn; *see* Tructwyn
Tully, 43
Tunbridge Wells, 33
Turin, 59
Turkey, 58, 61 *et seq.*
—— Company, 57 *et seq.*
Tuscany, Grand Dukes of; *see* Ferdinand *and* Cosimo

Tuscany, Princes of; *see* Leopold *and* Mattias

Universal Medicine, a, 8, 10

Van der Broechius, Adrian, 24, 42
Van Helmont, Baron Francis Mercury, 10 *et seq.*, 59, 65
—— —— Jean Baptiste, 11
Van Hoogstraaten, S., 21, 51
Vani Effendi, 68
Venice, 61
Vermaasen, John, 35 *et seq.*
Vesalius, 13; *Anatomy* of, 79
Veslingius, 13, 84
Vesuvius, 41
Virgil, 70

Waller, Richard, 23
Walton, Izaak, 4
Ward, 63, *quoted* 3, 73
Whaddon, Cambridgeshire, 1
Whichcote, Christopher, 48
—— Doctor, 48
—— Elizabeth; *see* Foxcroft, Mrs
—— Mary; *see* Worthington, Mrs Mary
William III, 44
—— IV, 52
Williamson, Secretary, 56
Winchilsea, second Earl of, 37, 42, 44 *et seq.*, 47, 55 *et seq.*, 61
—— tenth Earl of, 7, 83
Windsor Castle, 52
Winter, Sir Edward, 48 *et seq.*
Wood, Anthony, *quoted* 2, 30 *et seq.*, 44
Worthington, Dr John, 9, 48, *quoted* 31
—— Mrs Mary, 48
—— Mrs Sarah, 9
Wren, Christopher, 32
Wylde, Captain Charles, journal of, 58, 60

Zaccarias, Armenian servant of Sir Thomas Baines, 71 *et seq.*, 81 *et seq.*
Zant *and* Zephalonia, enquiries as to earthquakes at, 62

CAMBRIDGE: PRINTED BY J. B. PEACE, M.A., AT THE UNIVERSITY PRESS.